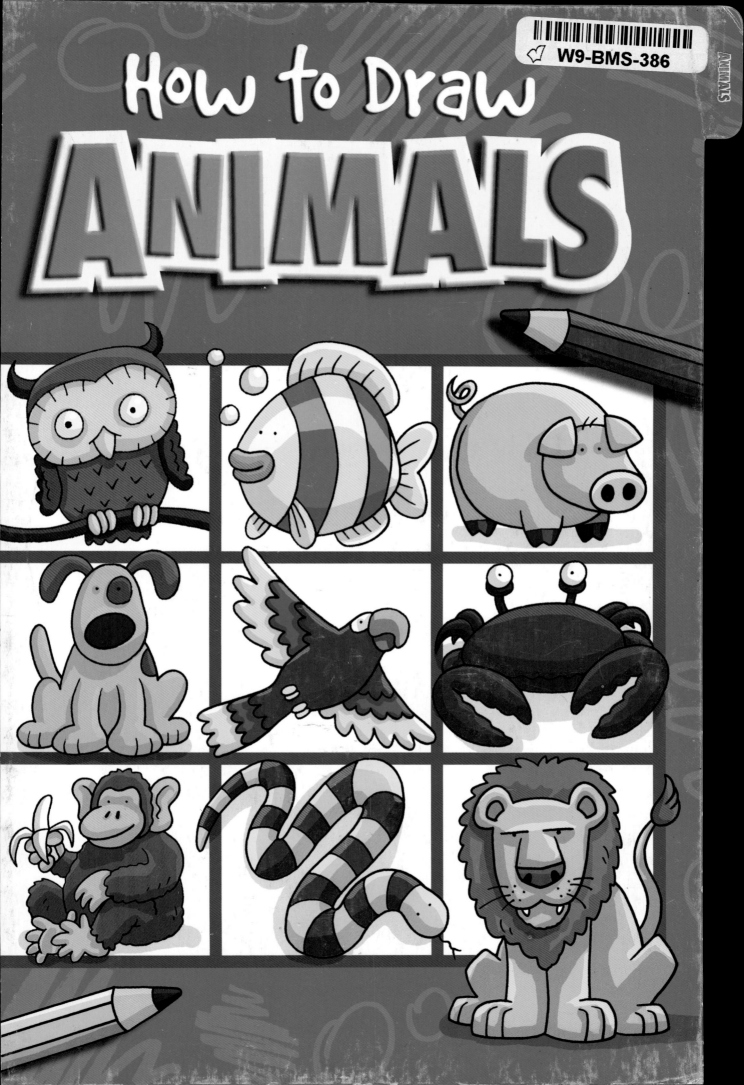

How to Draw
ANIMALS

ANIMALS

Lion

Pig

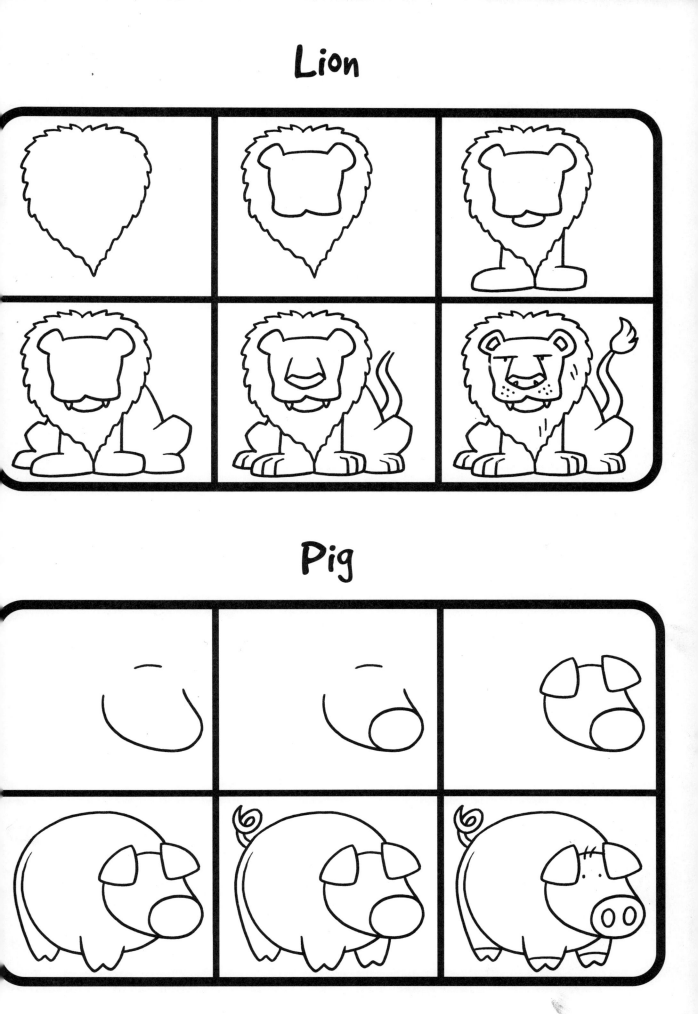

Lobster

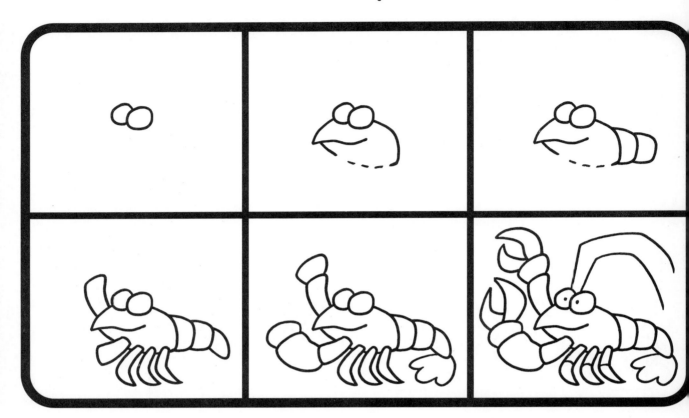

Kangaroo

Eagle

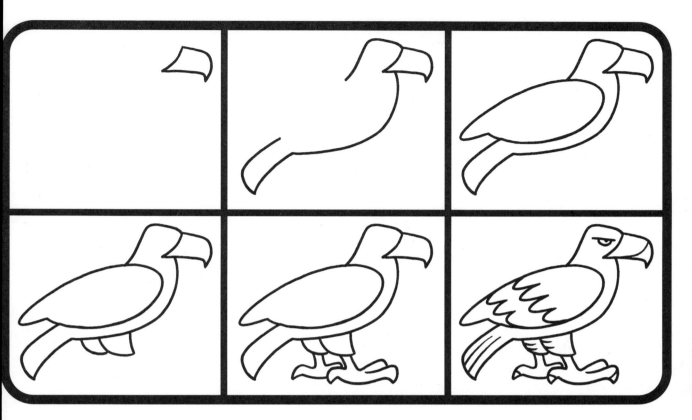

Chimpanzee

cat

Turtle

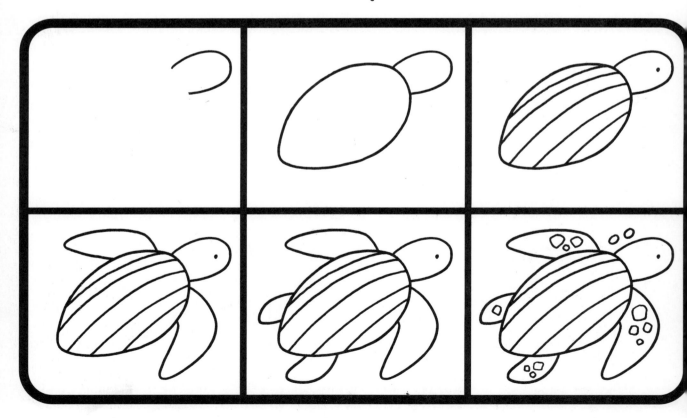

Dog

Baboon

Fish

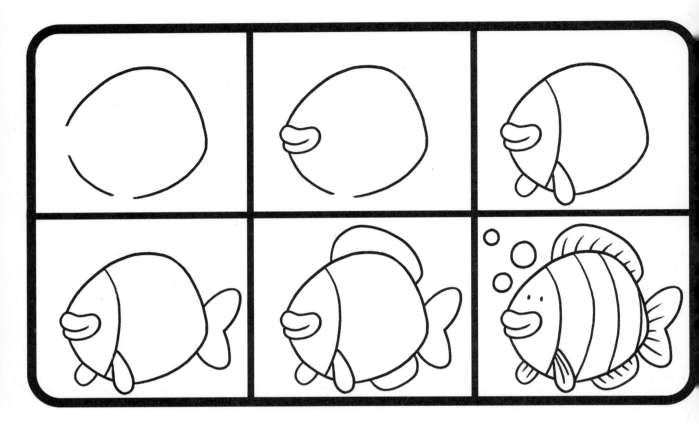

Tiger

Hedgehog

Kiwi

Parrot

Beetle

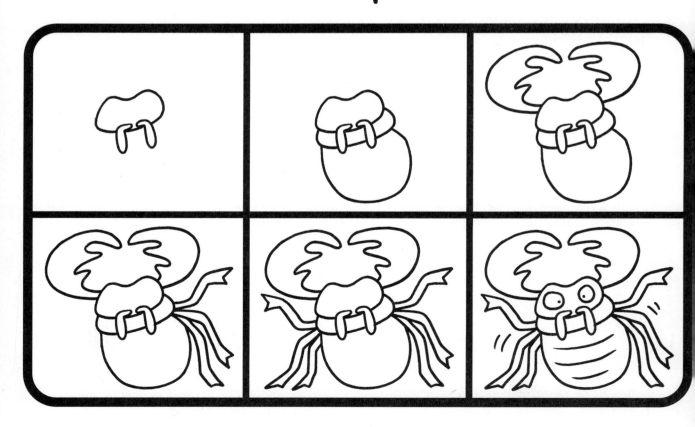

Anteater

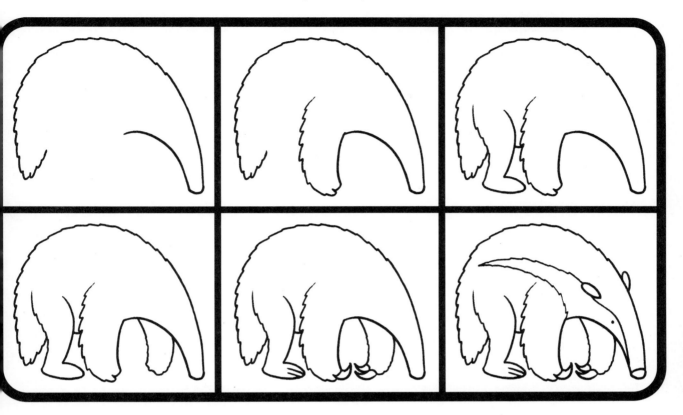

chicken

Budgie

orang-utan

Rhino

Bat

Squirrel

Donkey

Toad

owl

crab

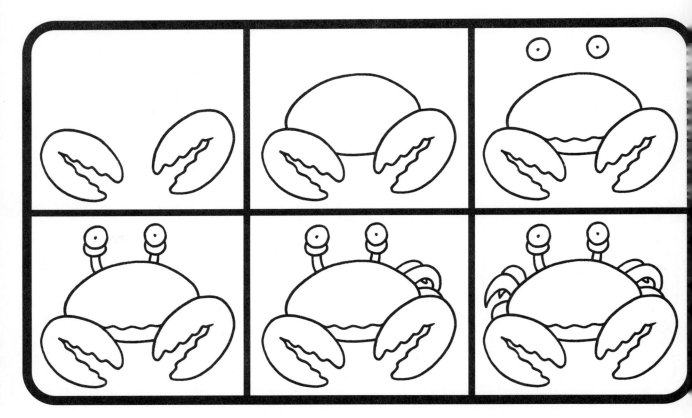

Dolphin

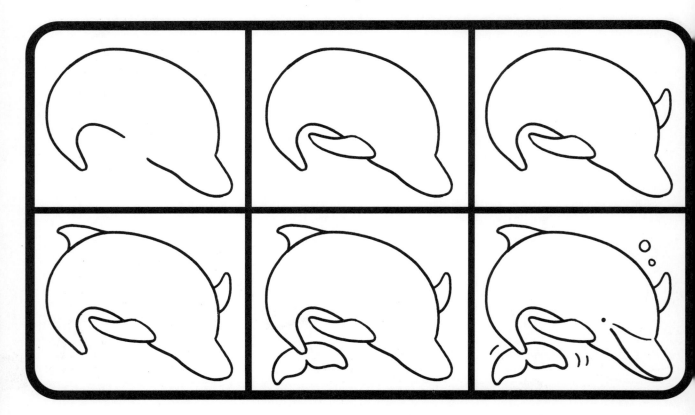

cow

Rat

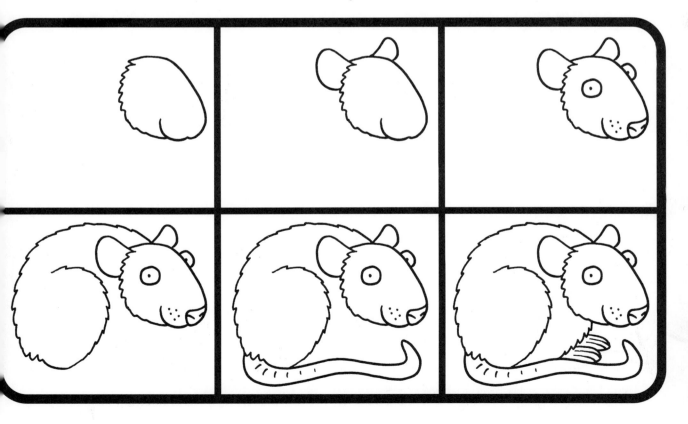

Seal

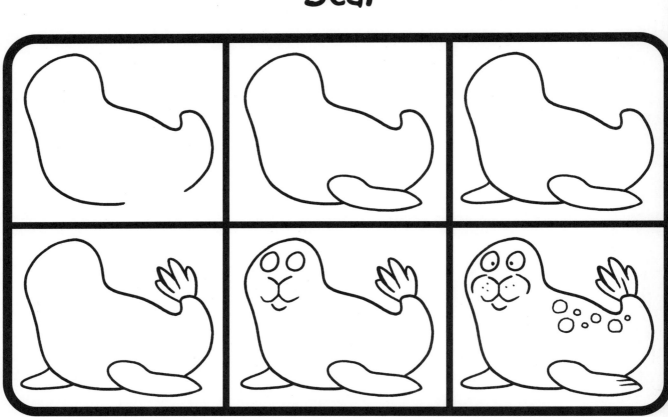

Tortoise

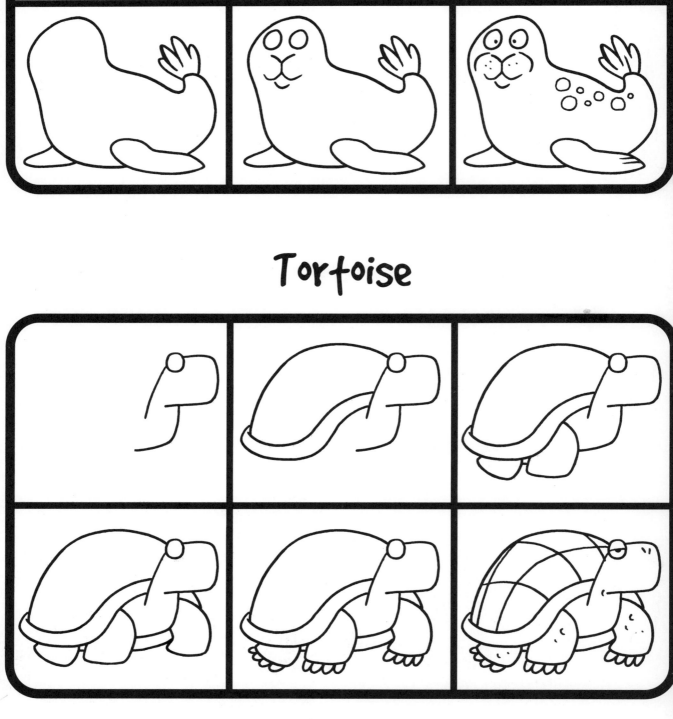

camel

Ant

Peacock

Jellyfish

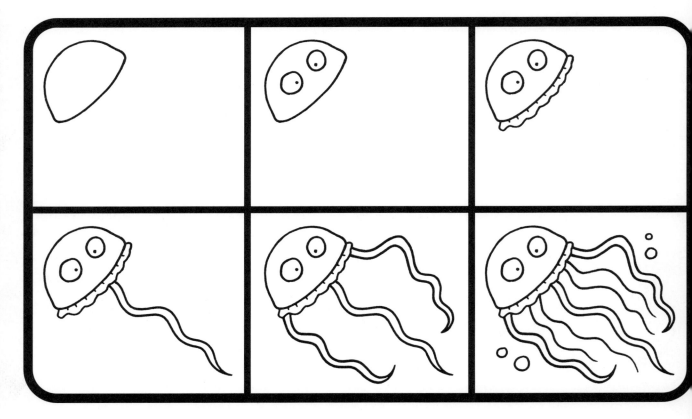

otter

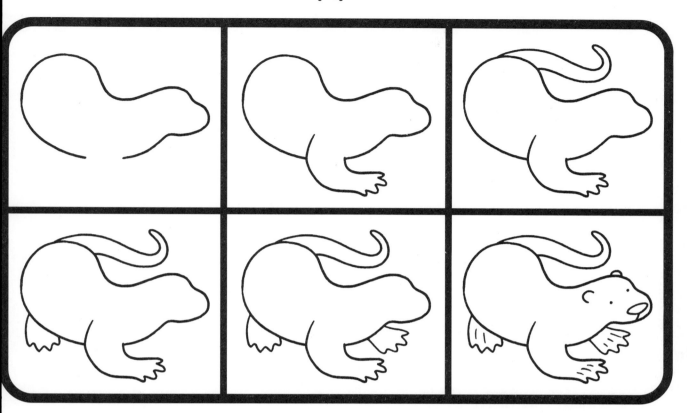

Zebra

Snail

Chameleon

Rabbit

Sheep

Panda

Snake

Killer Whale

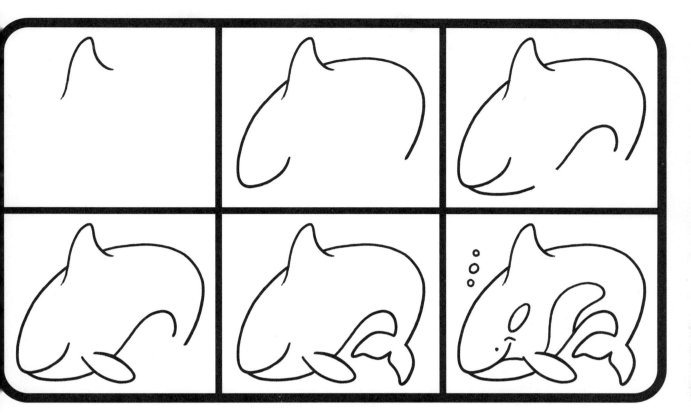

Toucan

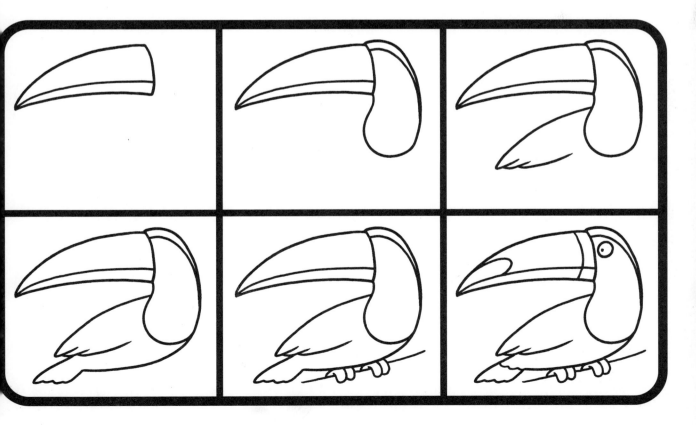

Lemur

Bison

Horse

Penguin

Elephant

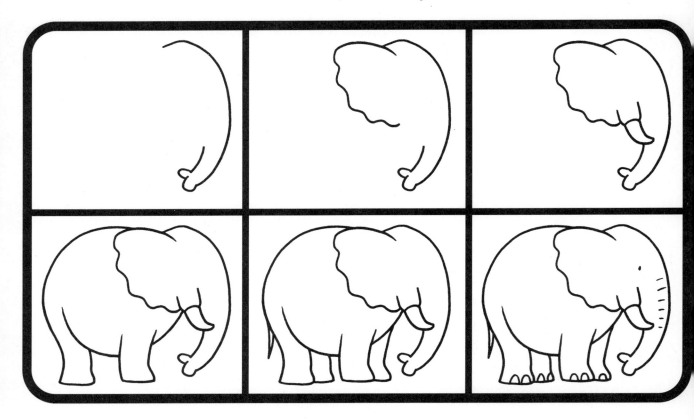

Frog

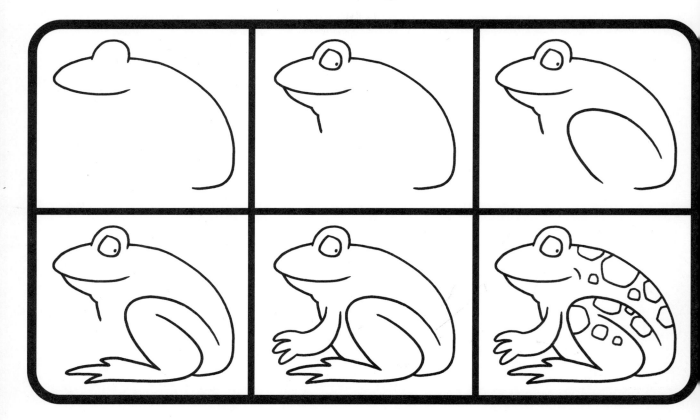

Shark

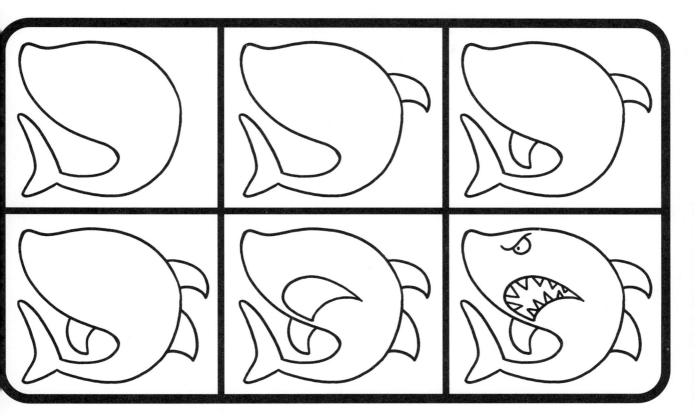

Goat

Panther

Kingfisher

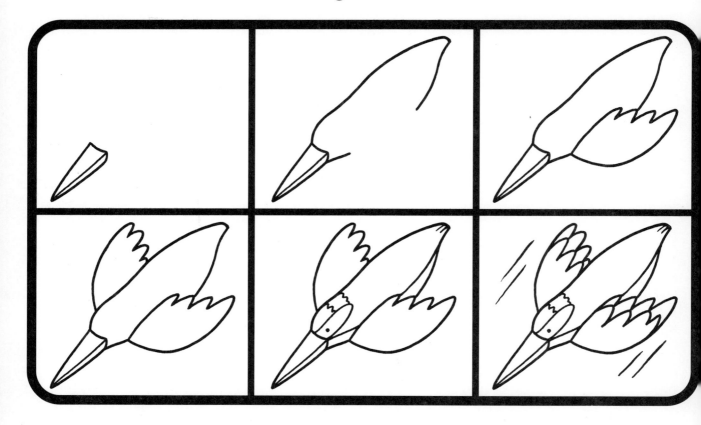

Grasshopper

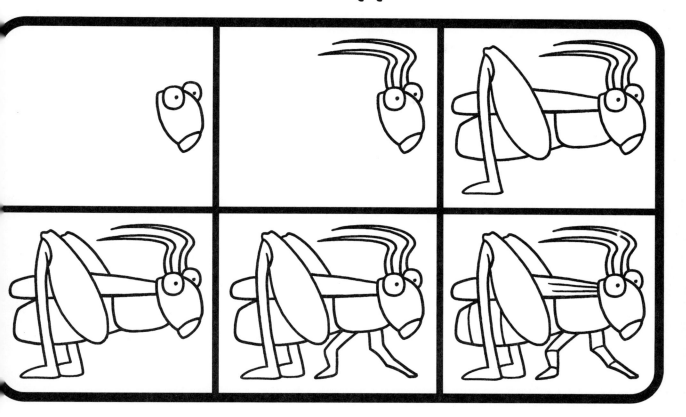

Squid

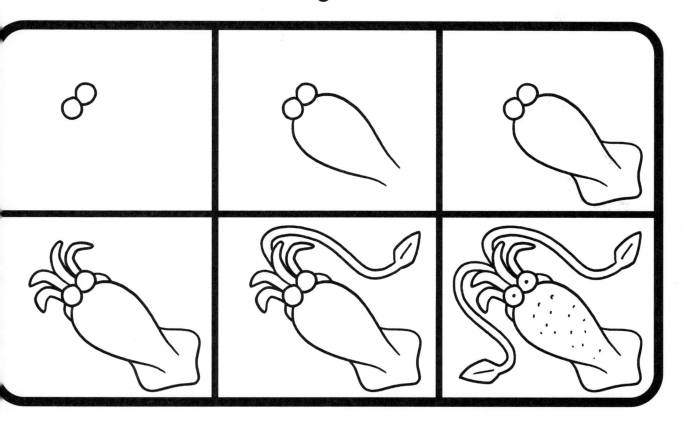

Duck

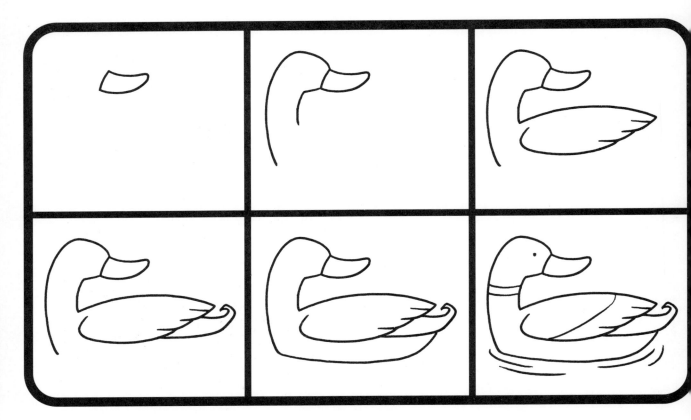

Porcupine

Humpback Whale

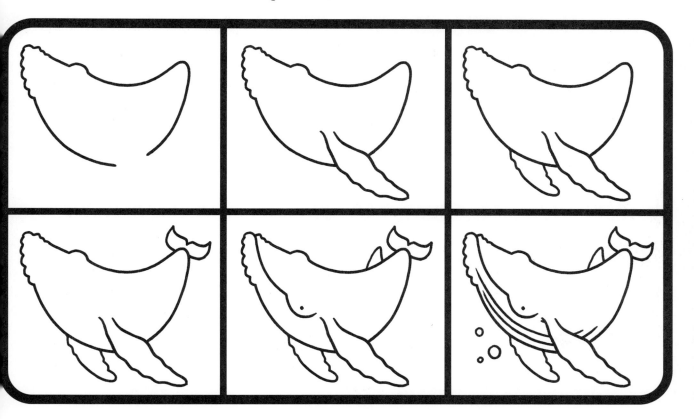

Beaver

Koala

Walrus

Roman Soldier

Baby

Roller Blades   Mechanic

Astronaut

School Girl

Astronaut

King   Queen

Doctor

Musician

Woman   # Man

Boy

Girl

old Lady   old Man

Pharaoh

Clown

Skateboarder   Greek Scholar

Infant

Judge

Greek Soldier

Victorian Lady

Teddy Boy   Teacher

Black Belt

Sailor

Tennis Player

Builder

Bride   Santa

Roman Emperor   Nurse

opera Singer   Sheriff

Artist   Witch

Dentist

Soccer Player

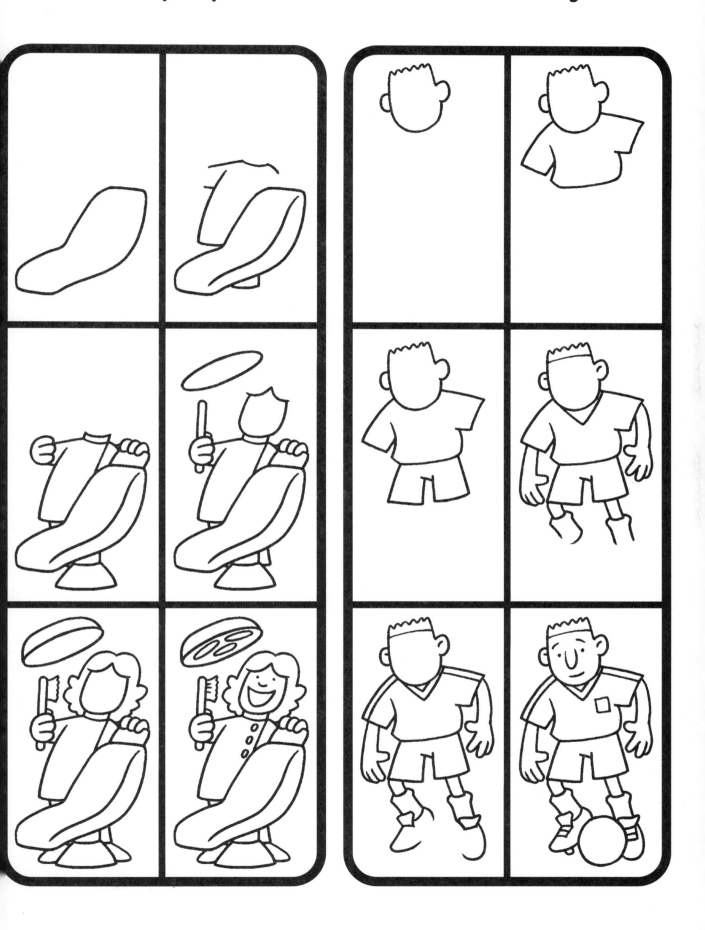

Ice Skater

Superhero

Diver　　　　Burglar

Chef   Elf

Cave Woman

Cave Man

Gardener　　Baseball Player

Fairy Baker

Tightrope Walker   Fisherman

Magician   Knight

Policeman

BMX

Rock'n'Roll Dancer

Postman

Deep Sea Diver

Wizard

captain

How to Draw
CARTOON CHARACTERS

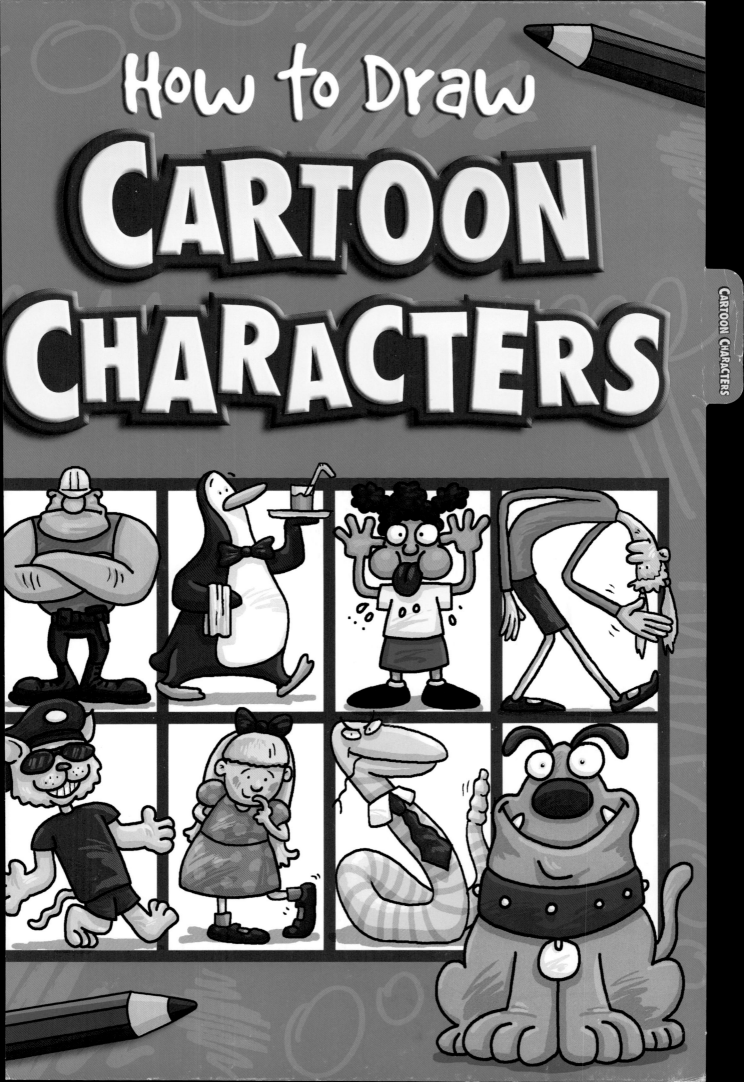

Rude Girl   Chef

Cup Winner

Skateboarder

Boxing Kangaroo

Caveman

Bendy Girl

Gangster

Wise owl

Hippo Ballerina

Penguin Waiter   Sneaky Snake

NFL Player

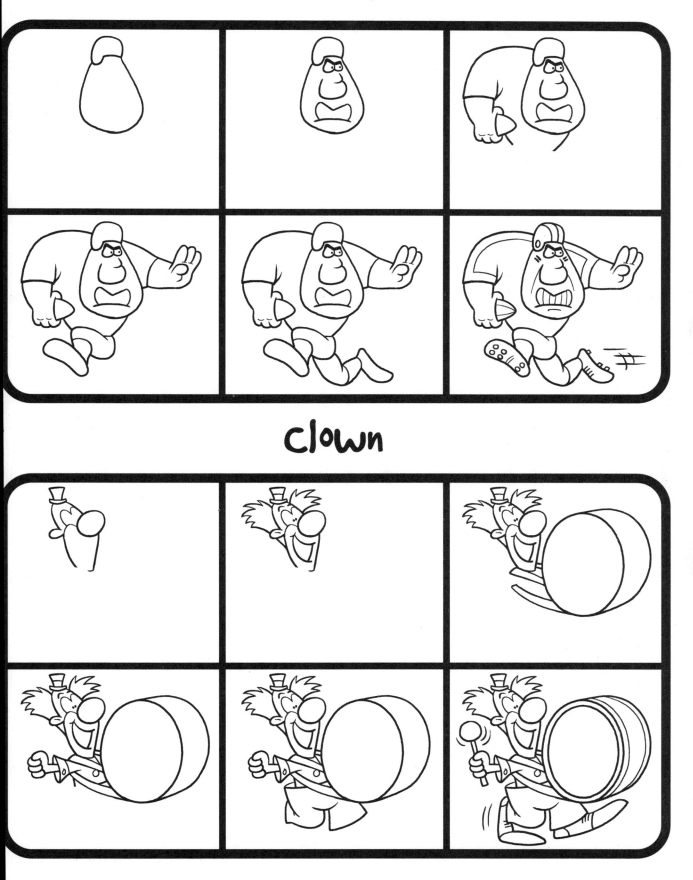

Clown

cycling Gorilla   # Dancing Pharaoh

Sweeping Girl

Cool Cat

Hula Girl

Big Builder

Angry Man

Daft Dog

Karate Girl

Scarecrow

Artist

Canoeing Moose

Tourist   Parachuting

Fun Ride

Dinner Bear

Screaming Girl   Tarzan the Tiger

Diver

Wet Dog

Deep Sea Diver

Party Girl

Easter Bunny

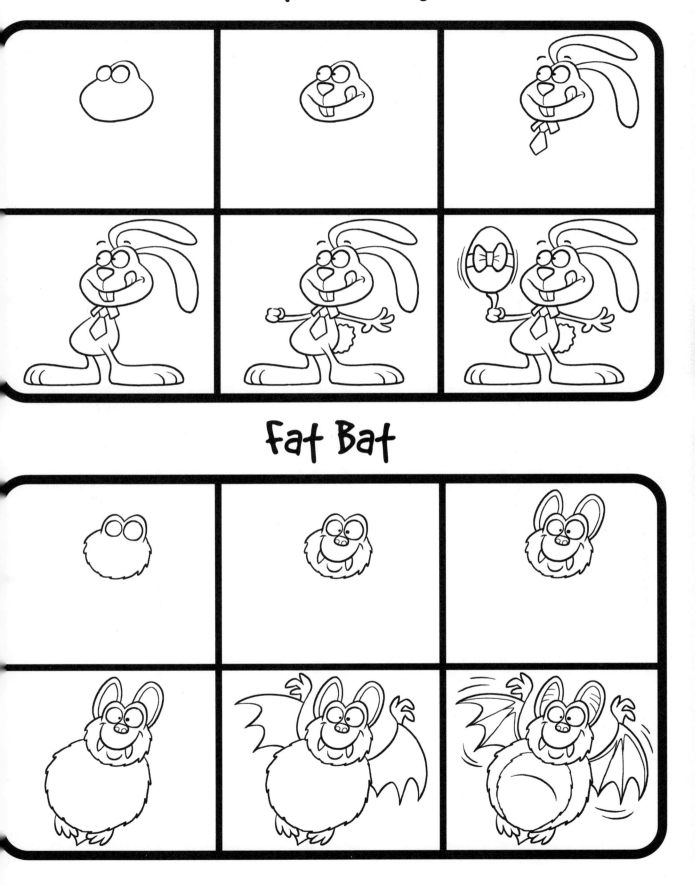

Fat Bat

Snowman   # Idea boy

Ghost

Flying Pig

Princess   Soccer

fisherman

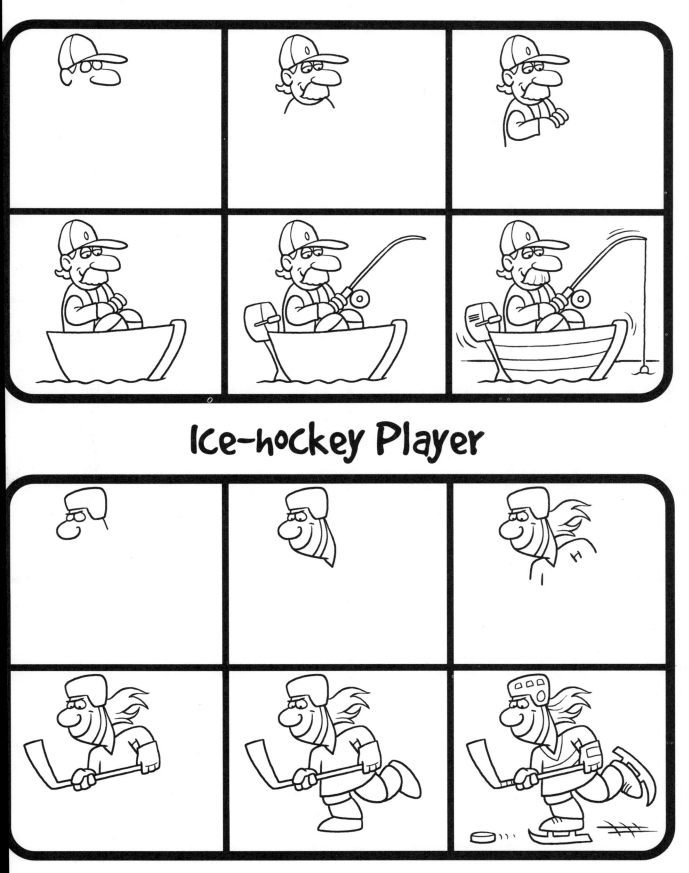

Ice-hockey Player

Thin Weightlifter

Jester

Kite Flying

Rhino on a Bike

Shy Girl   Surgeon

Body Builder

old Man

freezing

Yo-yo Boy

Skating Bear

Reindeer

crying Baby

Duck Spy

Knight on Horseback

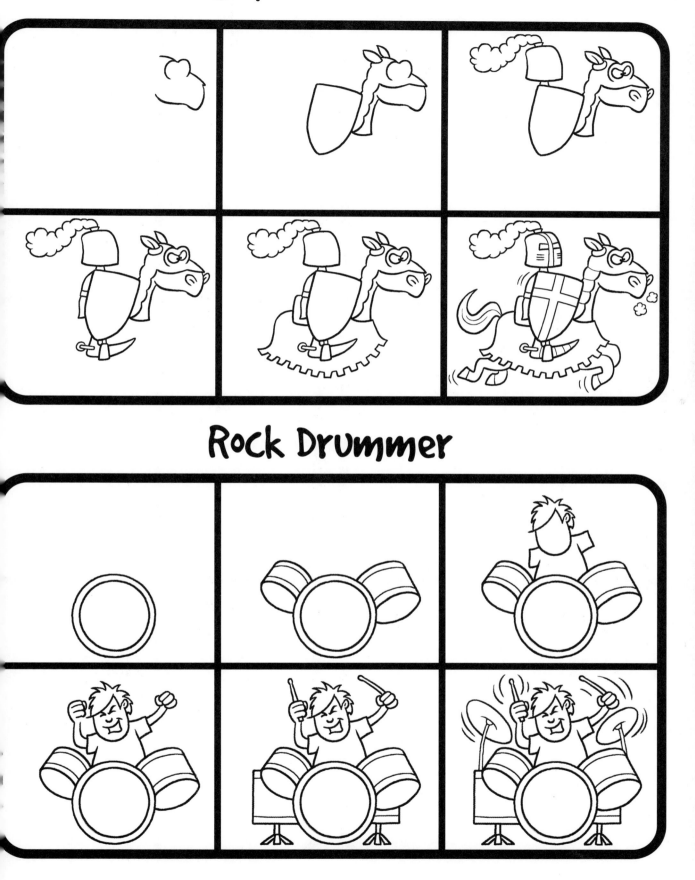

Rock Drummer

Hiker

Space-hopper Girl

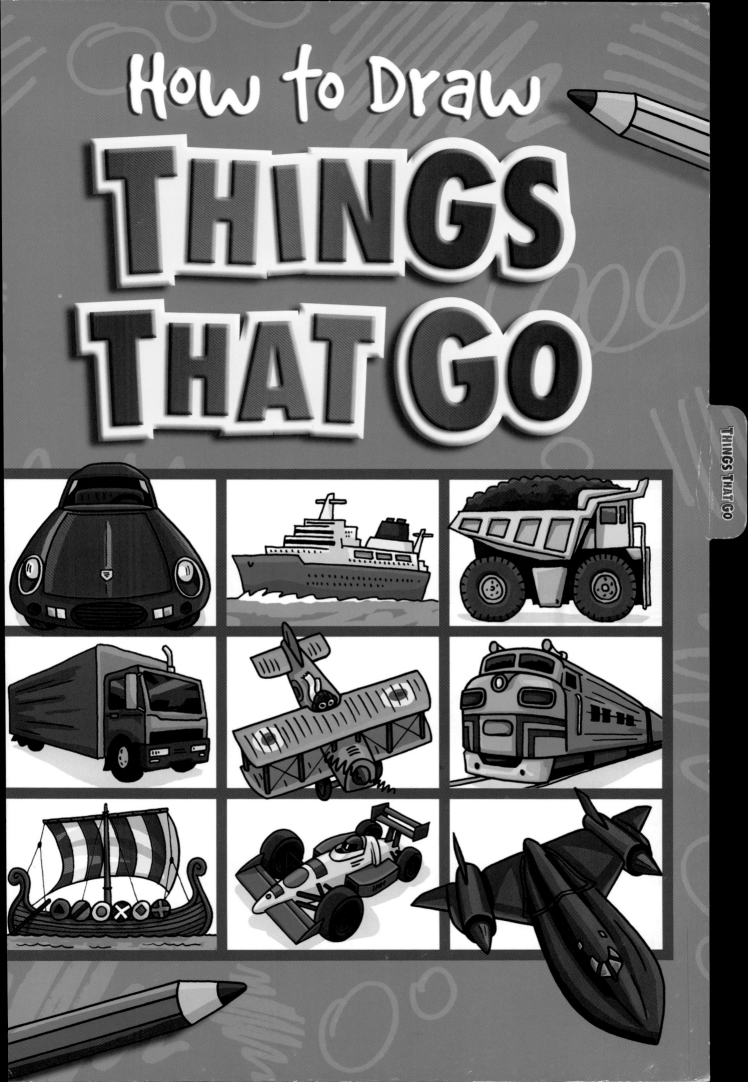

1960s Racing car

Viking Longship

freight Train

Spy Plane

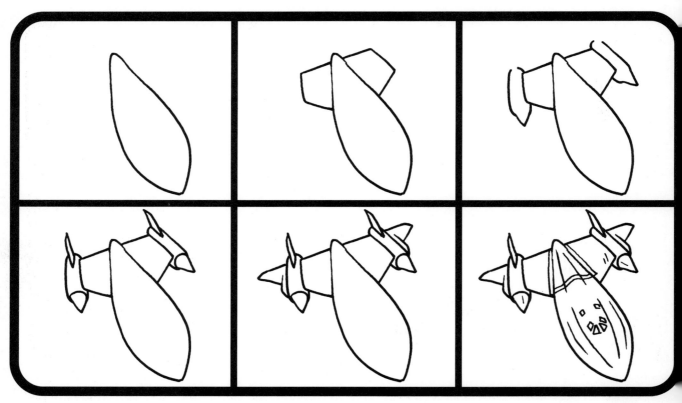

Racing car

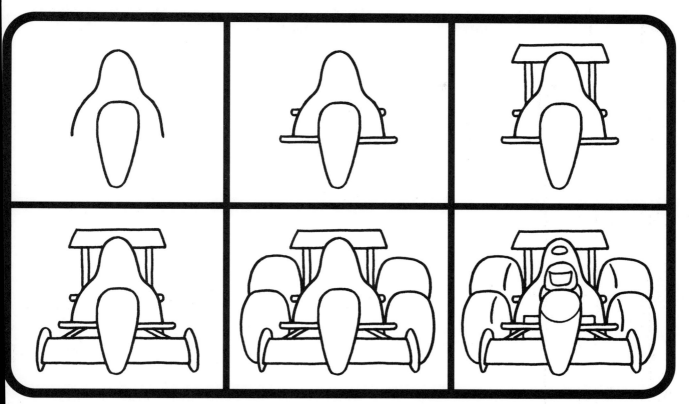

Tarmac Roller

cruise Ship

custom Bike

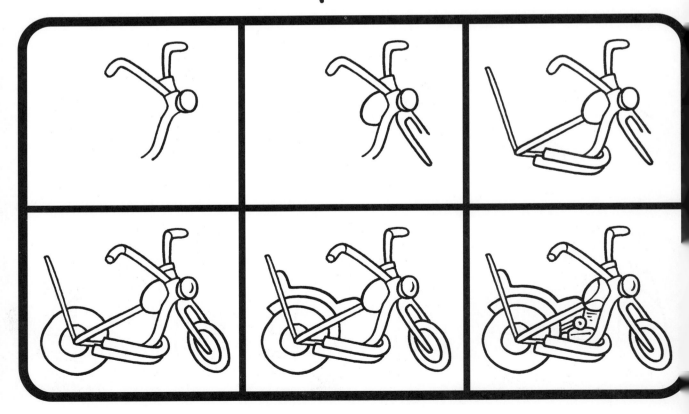

747 Jet

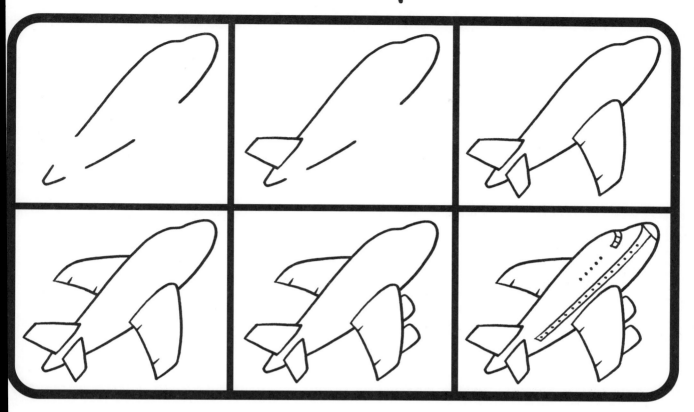

Custom Car

Mini

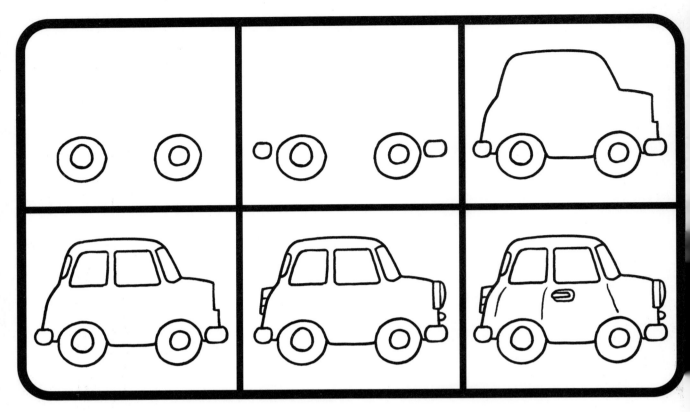

Digger

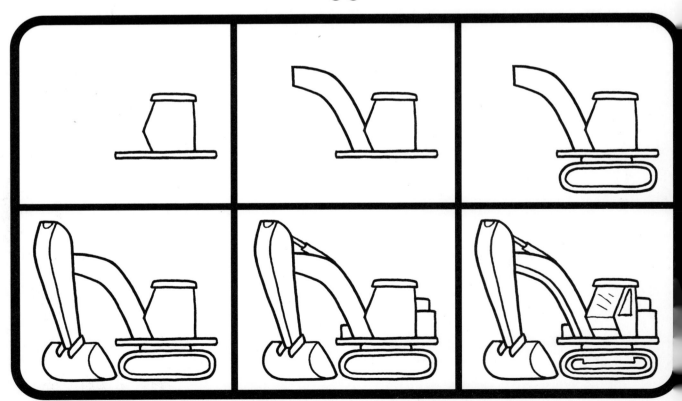

Lifeboat

Helicopter

Snow Ski

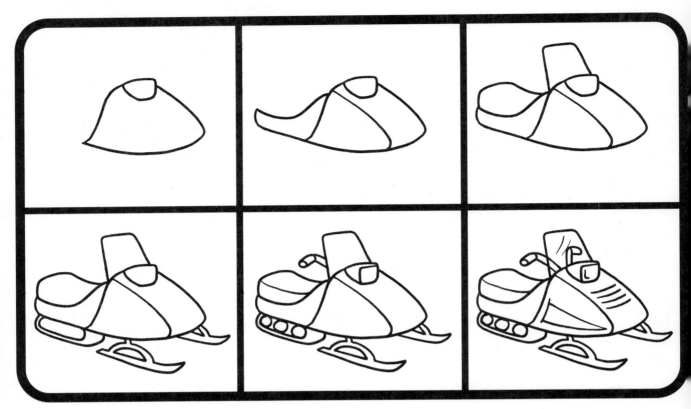

Moon Buggy

Crane

High Speed Train

Harvester

Racing Motorbike

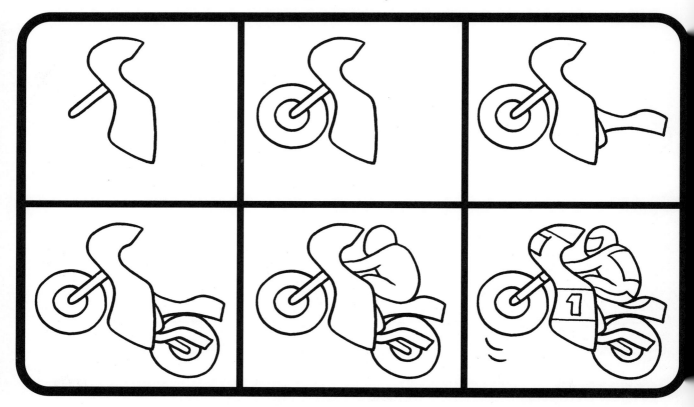

Police car

Wright Brothers' flyer

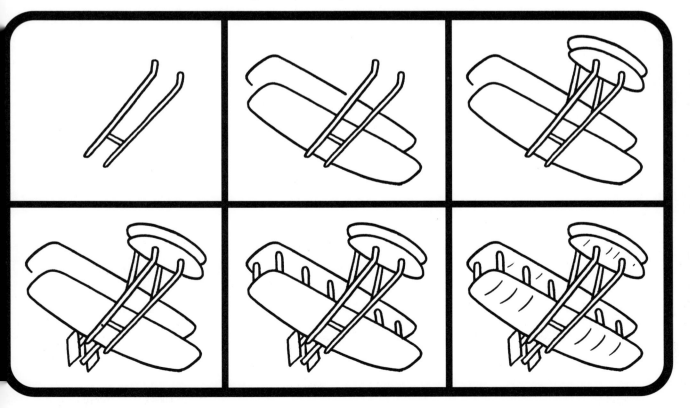

Mini Digger

Jet Ski

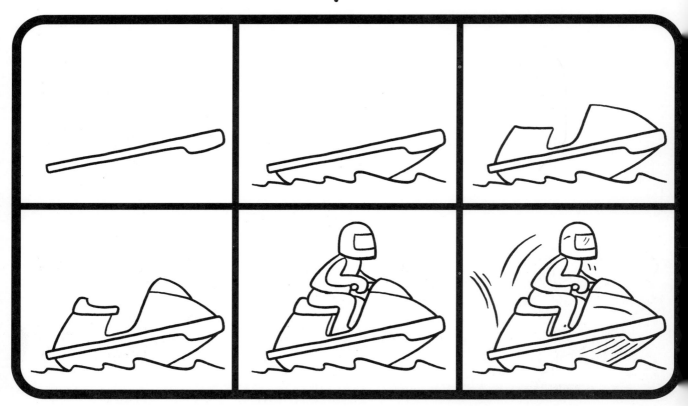

Space Shuttle

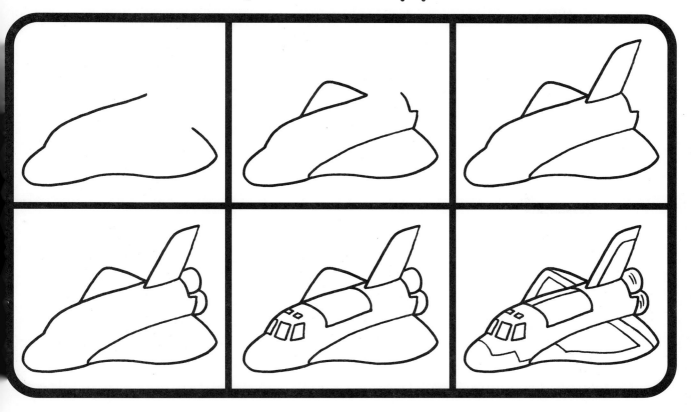

Junk Ship

off-Road car

Bullet Train

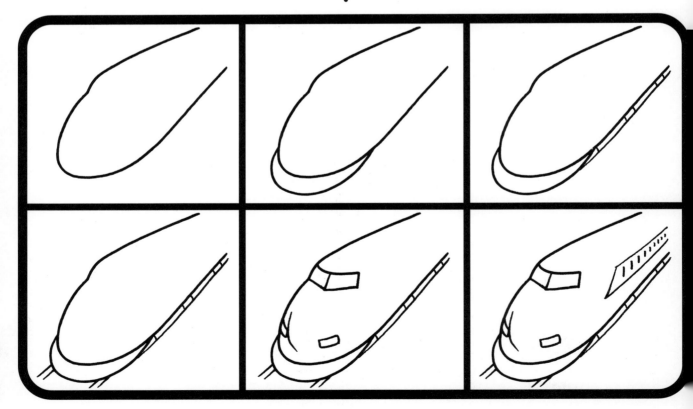

Motorbike

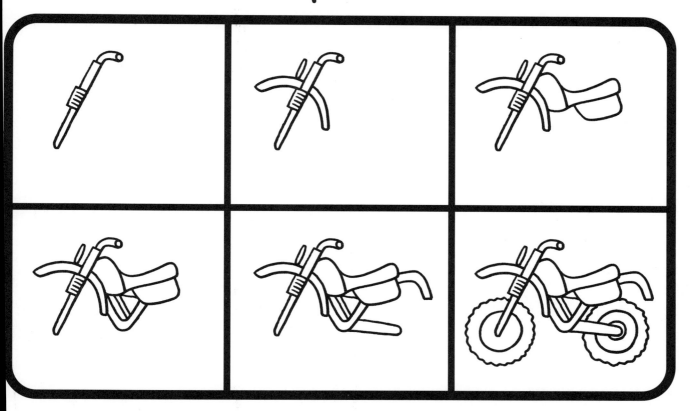

Traction Engine

Stealth fighter

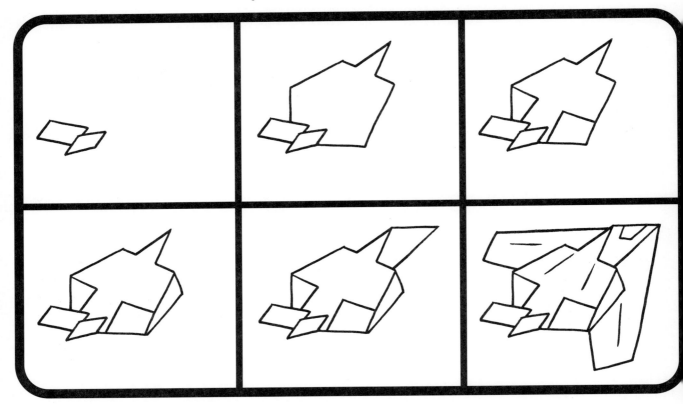

The first car

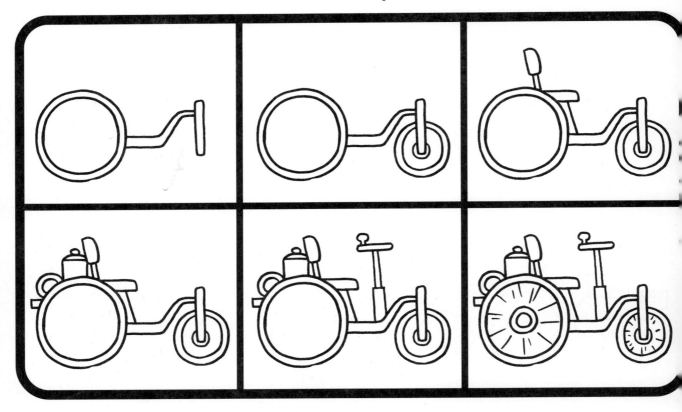

Dumper

cadillac

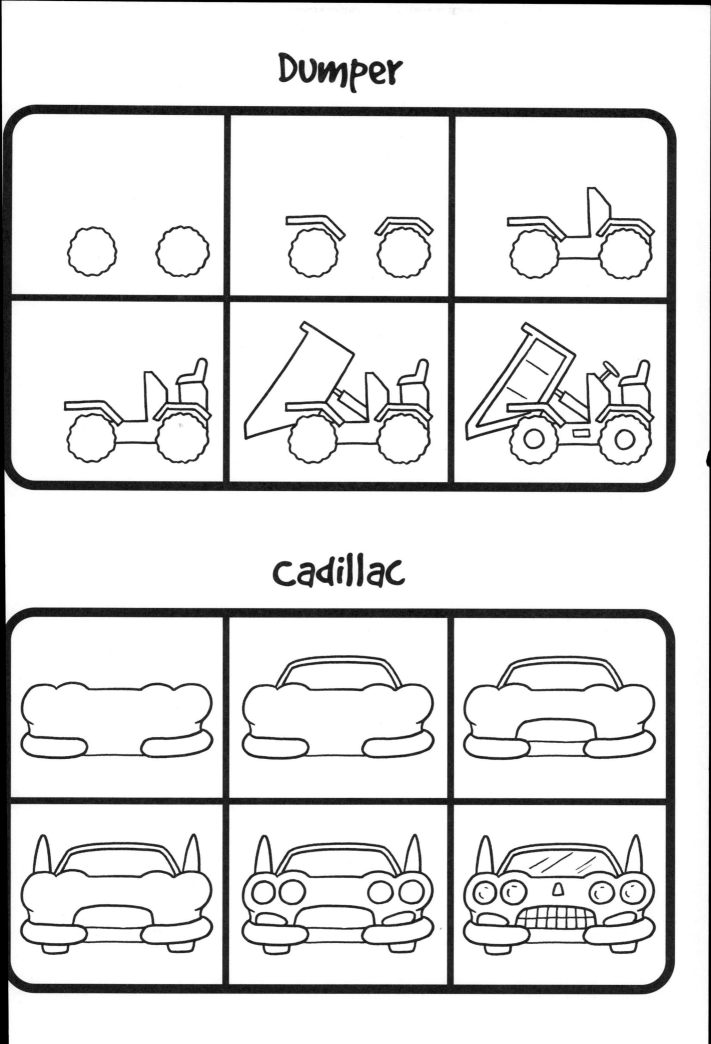

Rickshaw

Hydro-foil

Snow Plough Engine

Spitfire

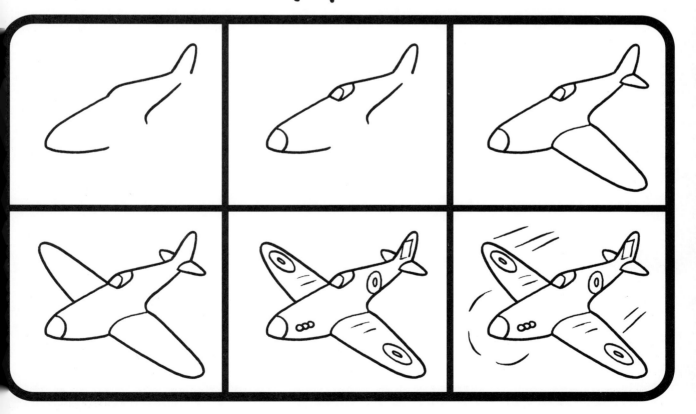

Bubble car

cement Truck

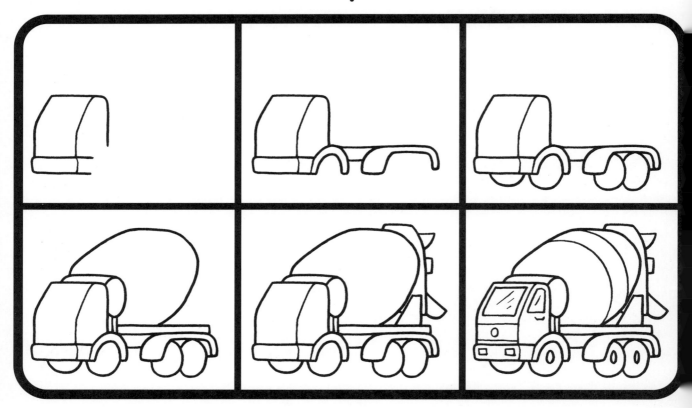

Microlight

Paddle Steamer

17th Century Ship

Monster Truck

Dumper Truck

Scooter

Le Mans Racing car

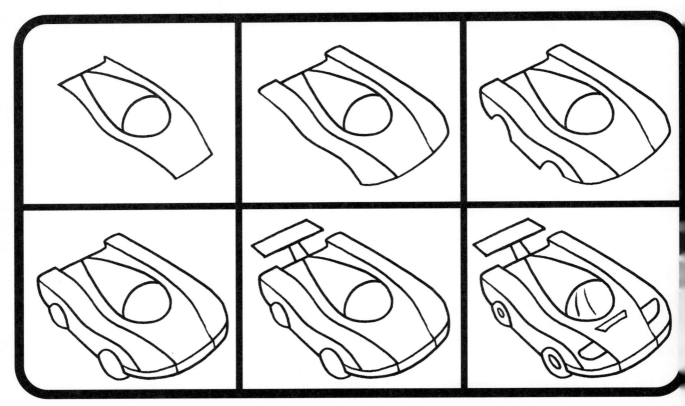

Skip Truck

Hovercraft

The Mallard Train

Roller

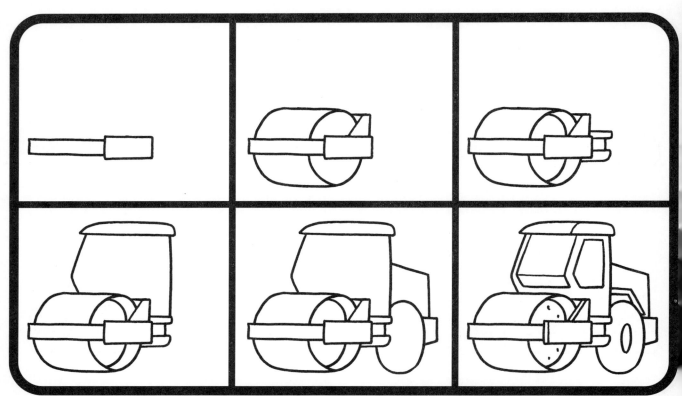

Fishing Boat

Utility Truck

Lorry

Speed Boat

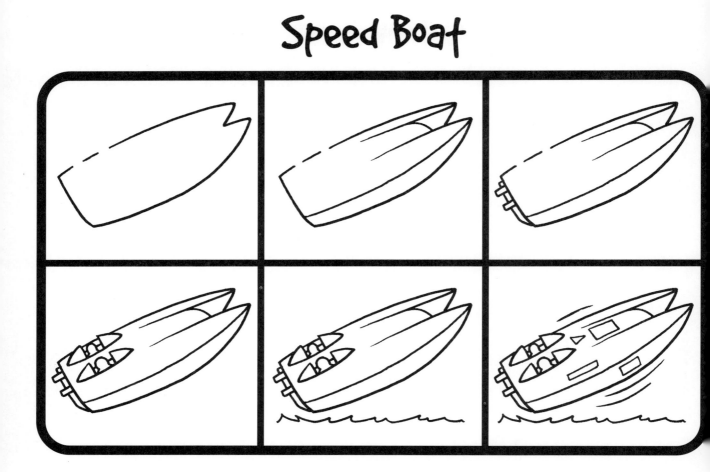

1901 oldsmobile

Sea Plane

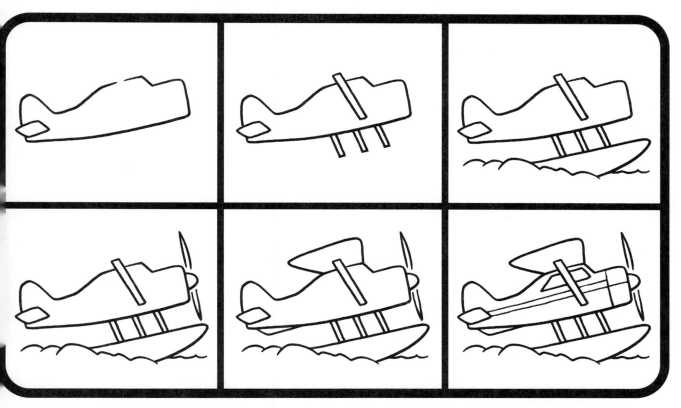

London Bus

Tractor

Snow cat

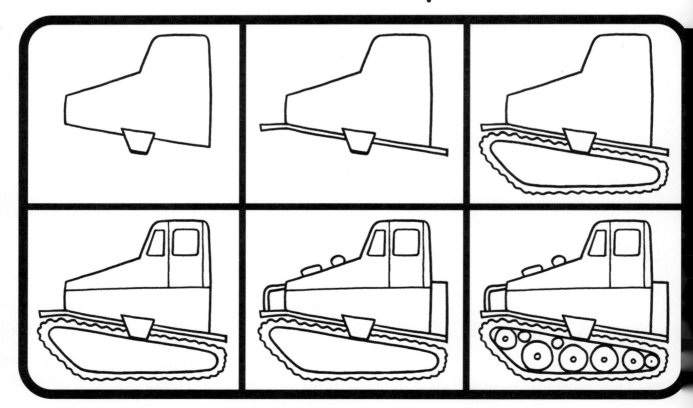

Fire Engine

Stock car

Submarine

Bi-Plane

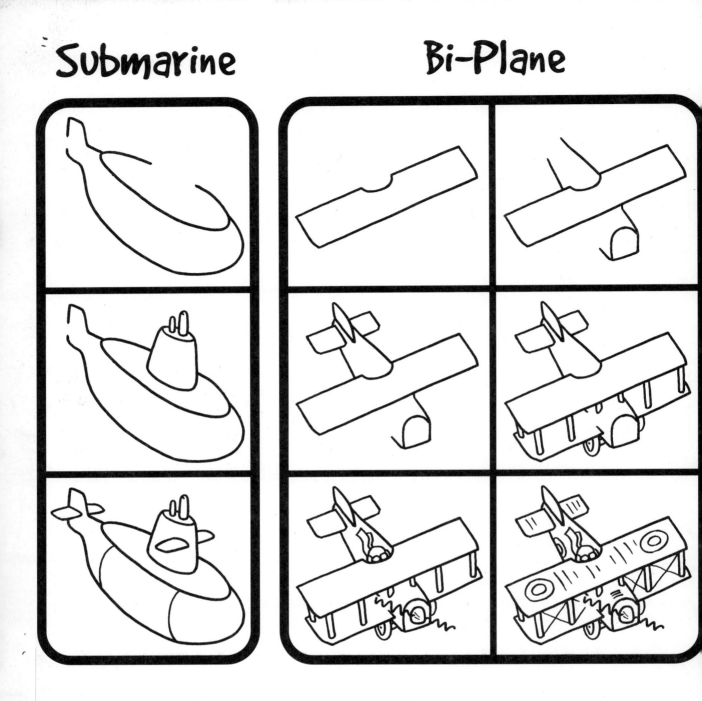

Monorail Train

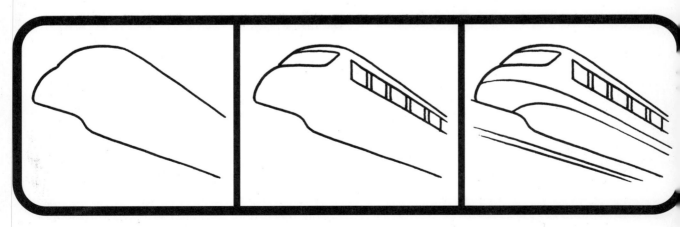

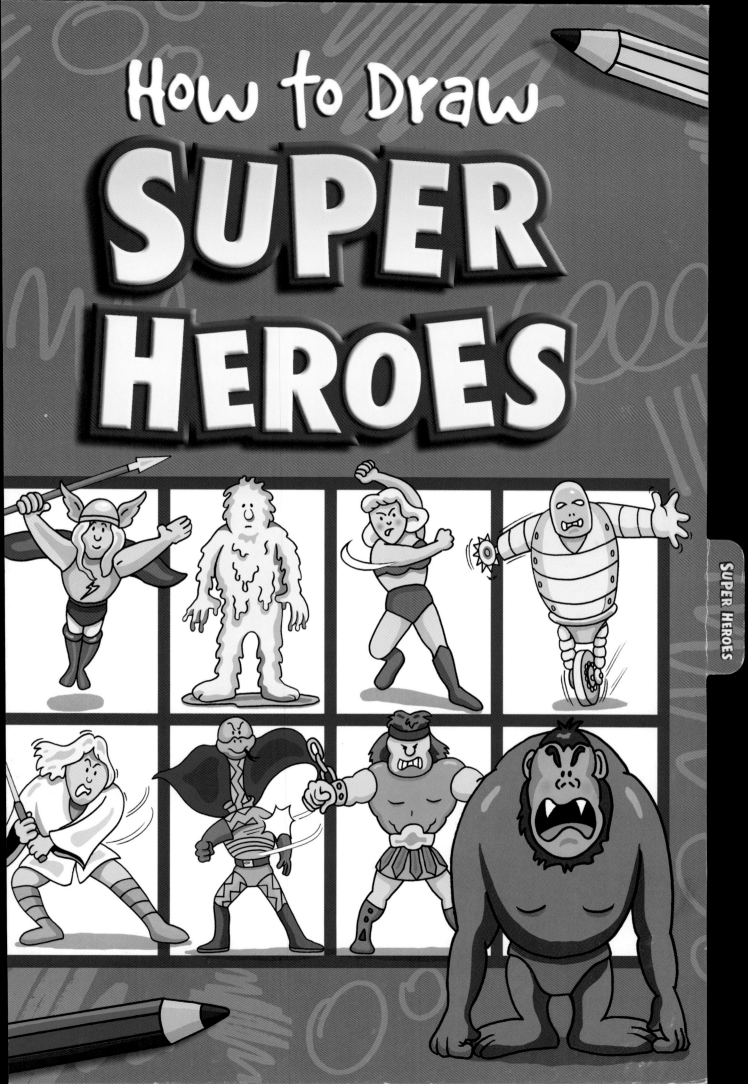

How to Draw
SUPER HEROES

Snakehead

Super Sleuth

Star Pilot

Super Bug

Super Gloo　　Princess Mighty

Super Lady   Jaws

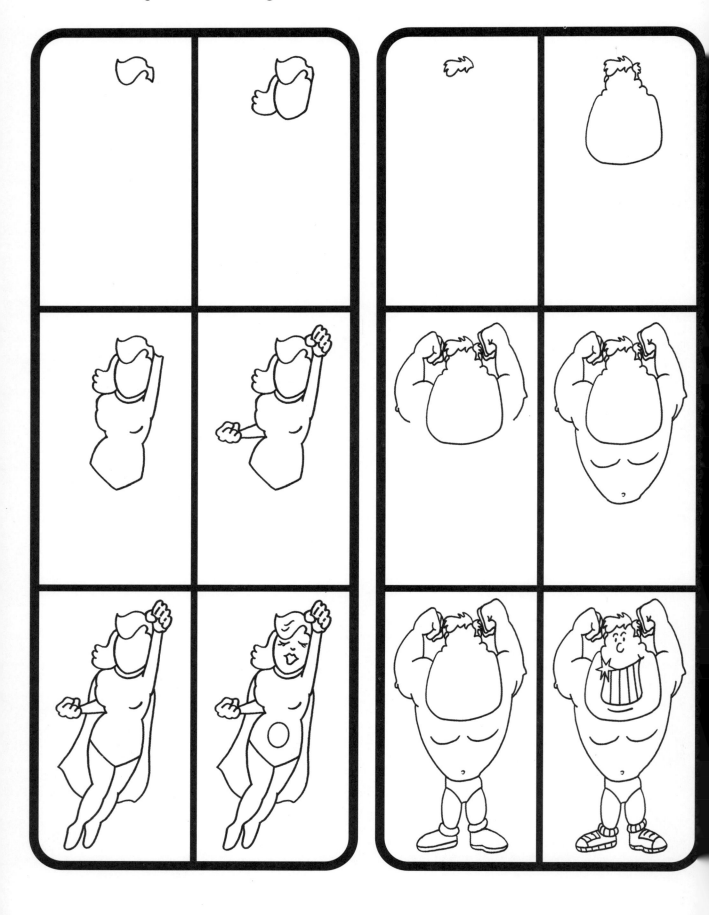

Super Thor

Super caveman

Blade Warrior   # celtic Warrior

Super cook   Jungle Man

Robin Hood

Dragon Queen

Sir-Lance-A-Lot

Hannibal

Super Duck   Hammer Head

Super Moose

Volgan

Buffalo Bill

Galactica

Super oil   Rope Breaker

The Bat

Globe Man

Space Robot   Space Baroness

Space Warrior   Sonic Hero

Mechanic Man   Demon Fighter

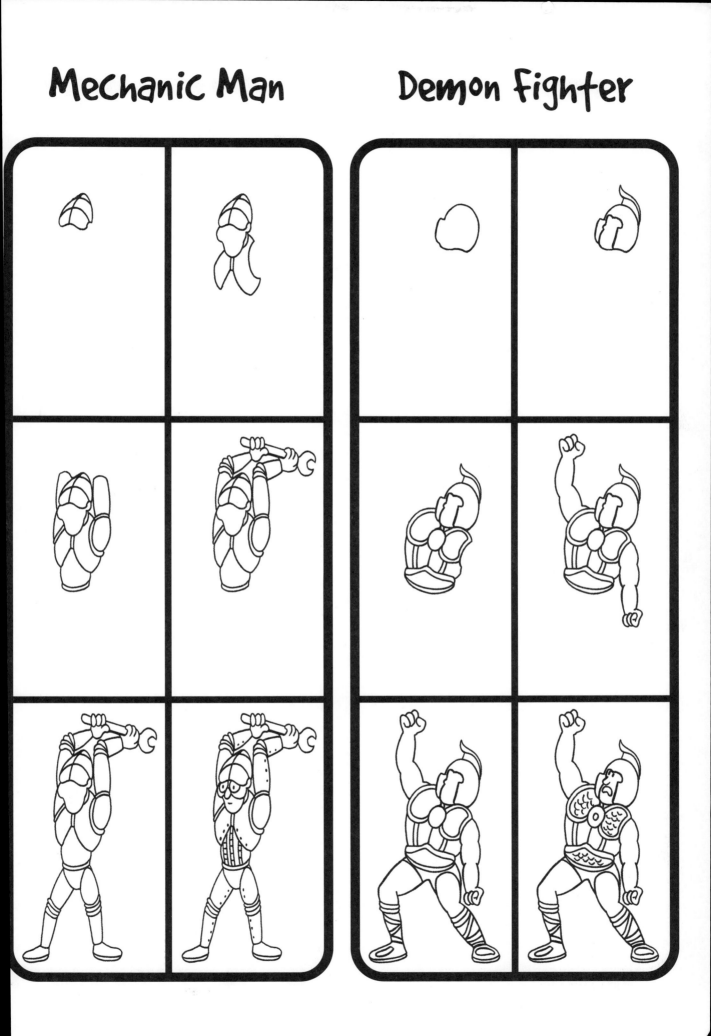

Demon Slayer　　Lightning Diver

UDDz

captain Galactic

Ninja   # Axeman

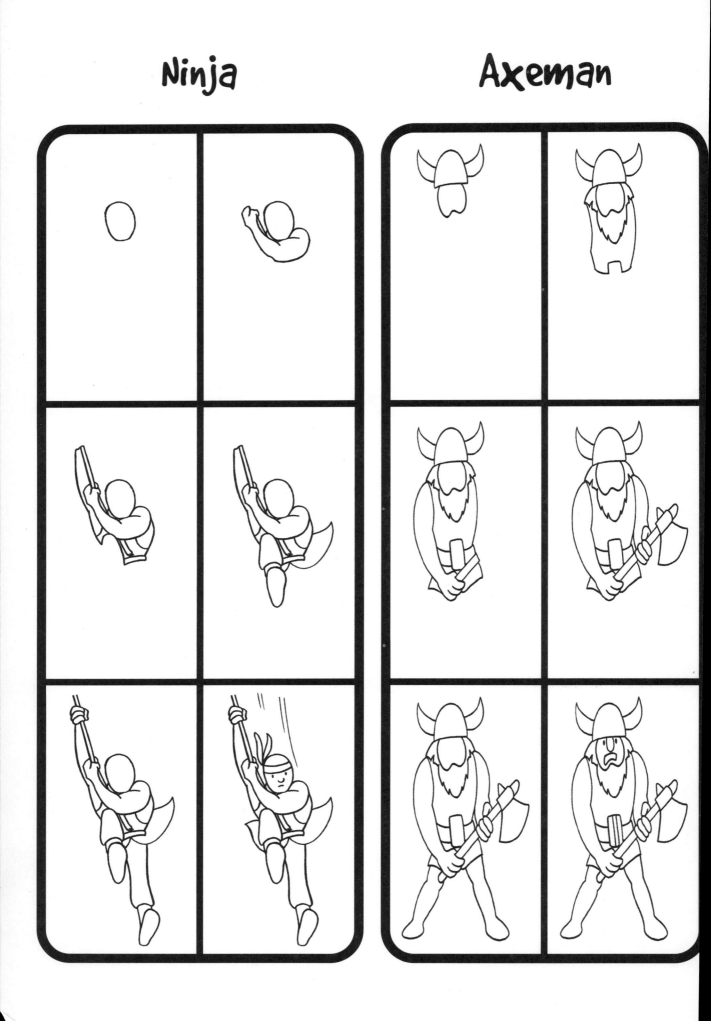

The Archer   Lightning

Sky Boxer   Venus Amazon

Star Warden

Spartacus

Star Hunter

Space Shield

Kajo

Zulu

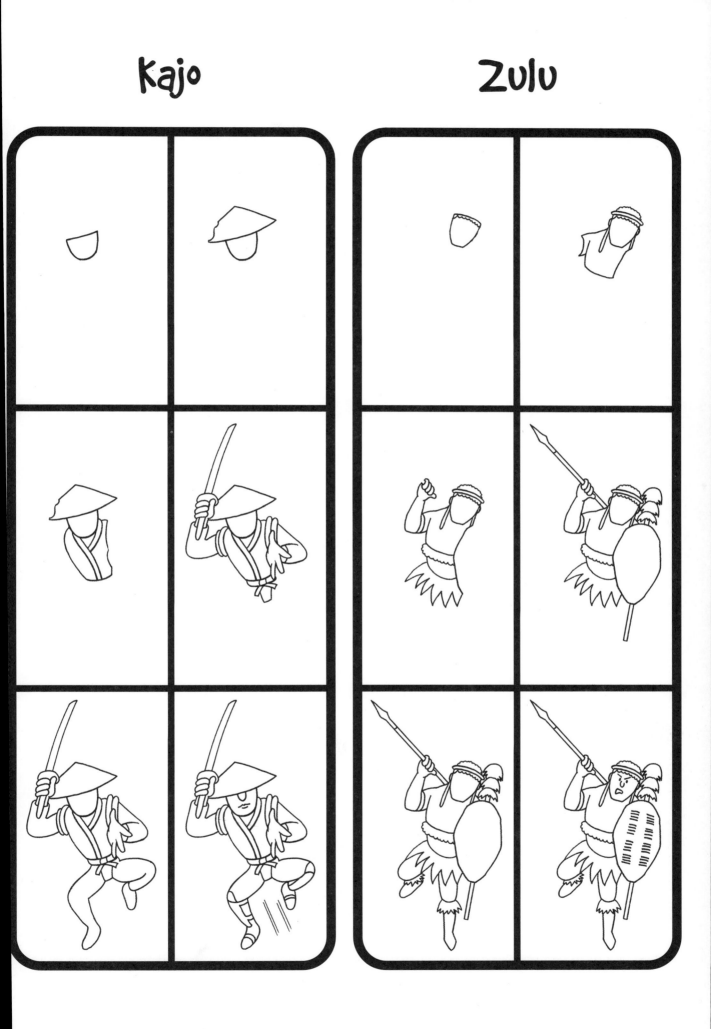

Robot Warrior

Frogman

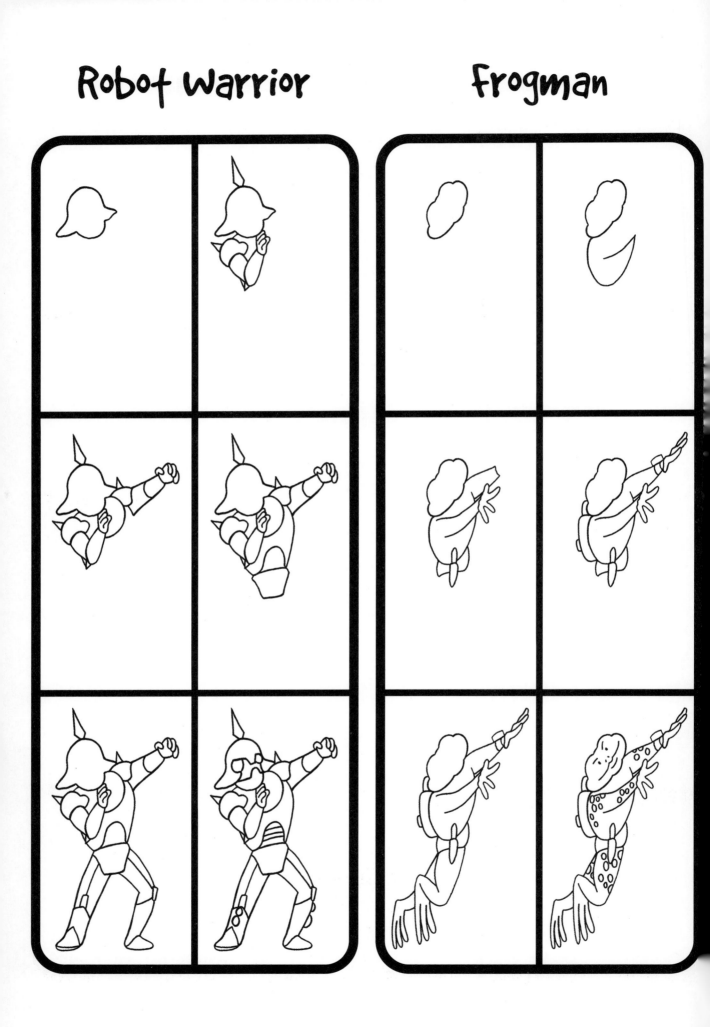

Space Sniper

Prince Sword

Karate King

Sky Diver

Super Saver

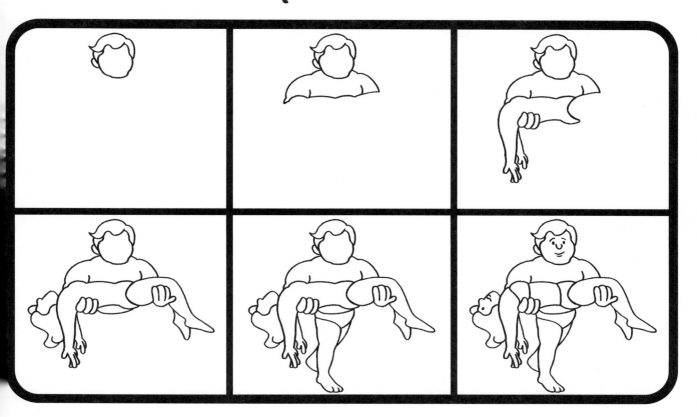

Layzar

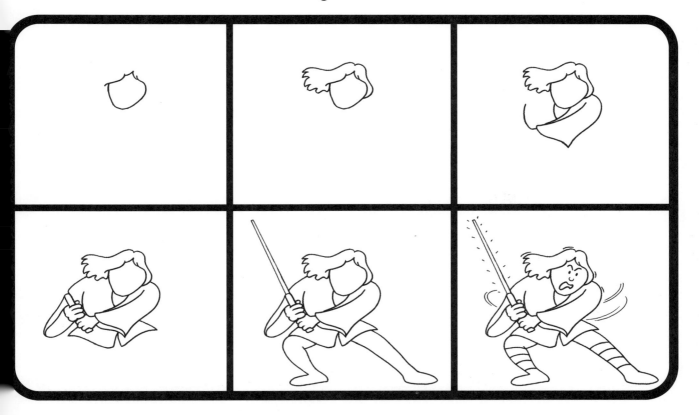

Queen Boudicca

Kongo

Super Star

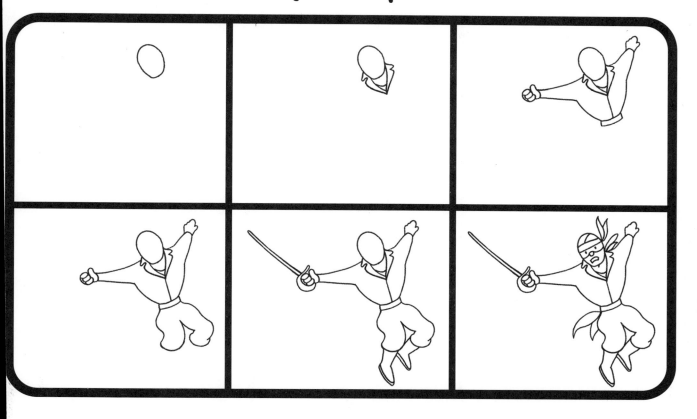

Sky Leaper

Iron Man

Super Spy

Goliath

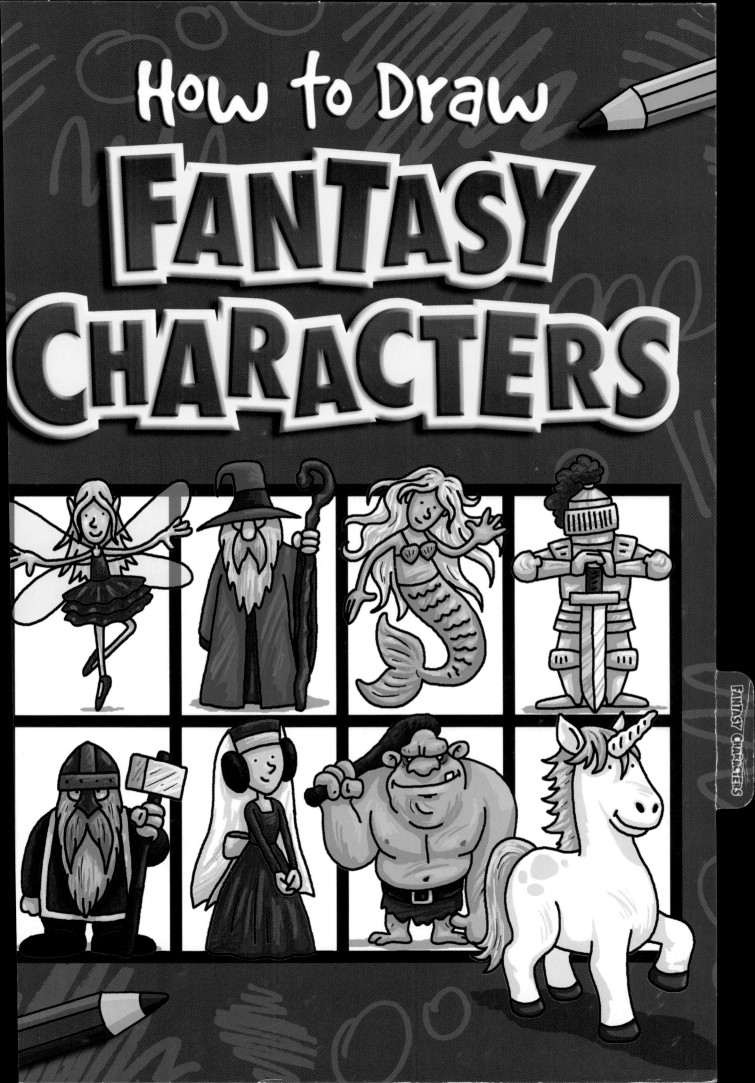

How to Draw
FANTASY CHARACTERS

fairy   wizard

Minotaur   House Goblin

Ice Queen   Yeti

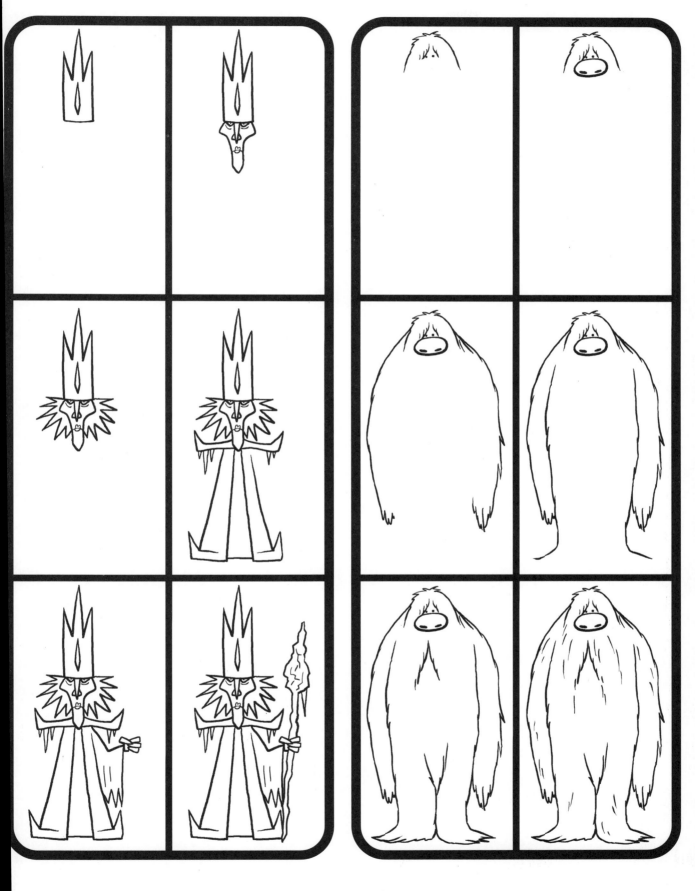

Knight   # Dwarf

Witch

Elf King

Phoenix

Gremlin

Mermaid

Dragon

Pixie   Zombie

Fairy Queen

Tree Man

Leprechaun

Swamp ogre

Alien   # Nymph

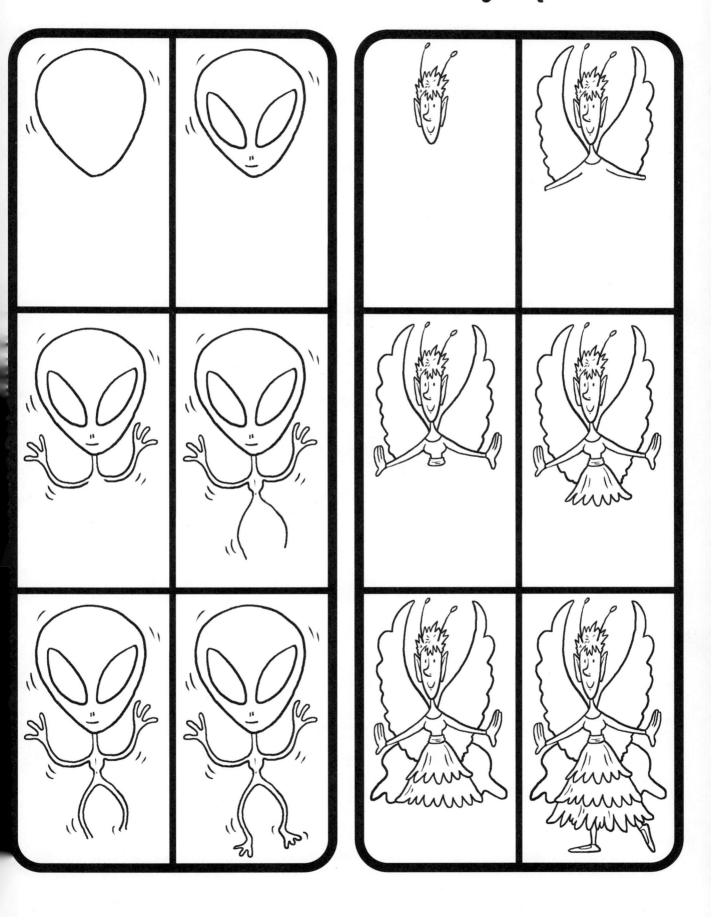

Pegasus

flot Smudger

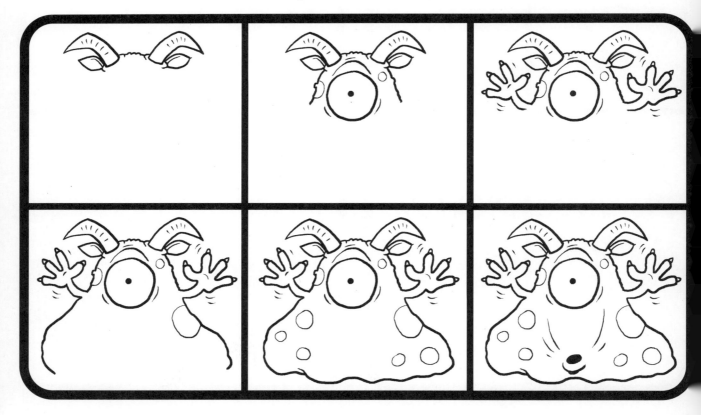

Two-headed Dog

Giant octopus

Grim Reaper

Prince Charming

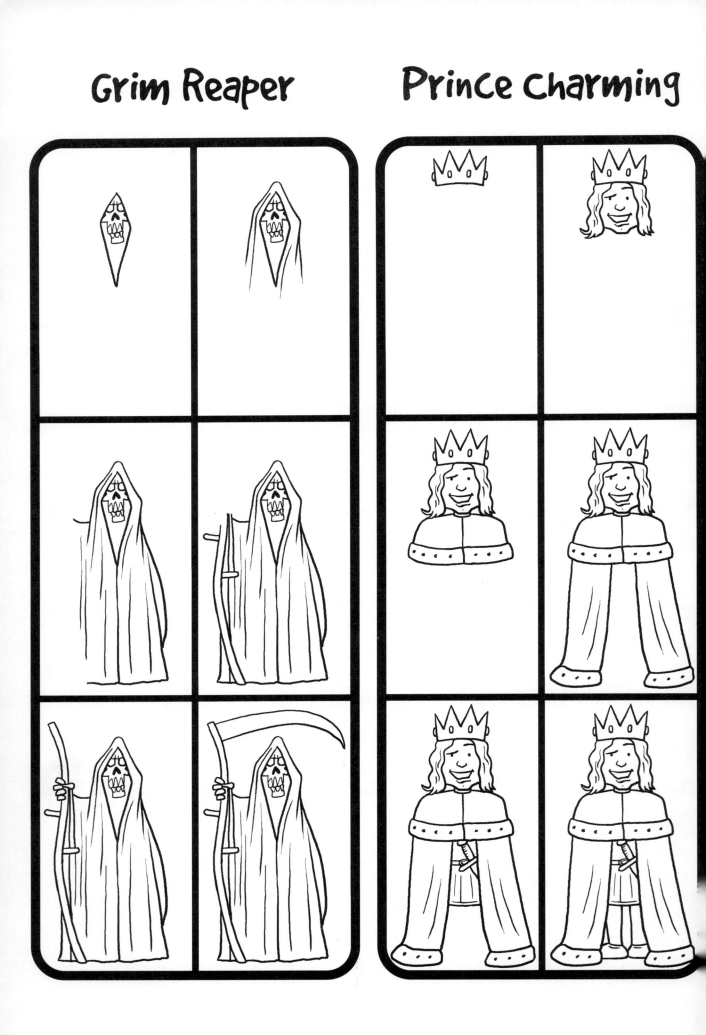

Jack Frost

Ice Queen

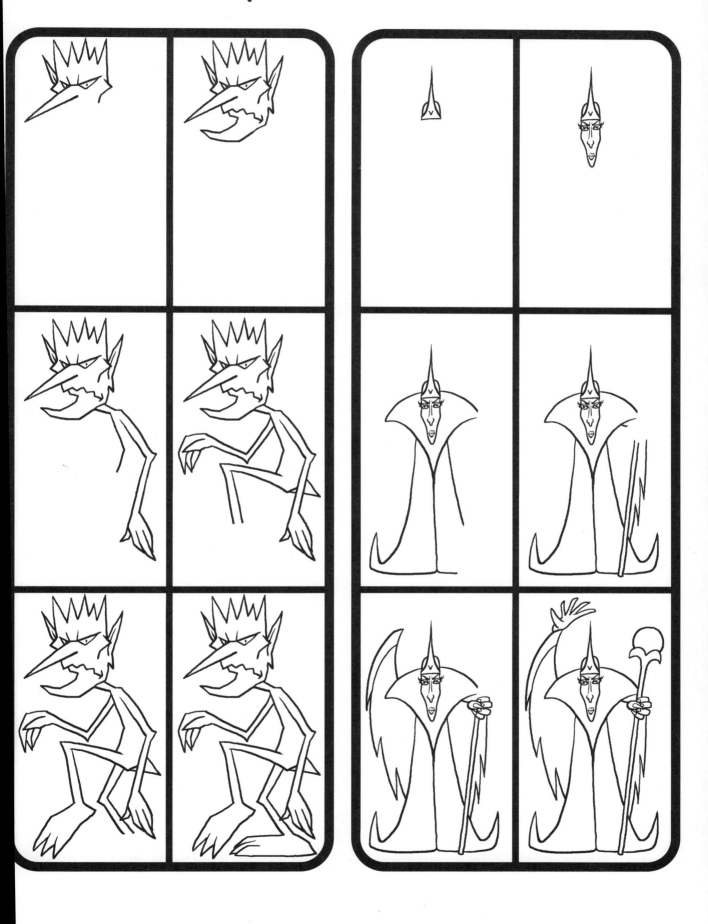

fraggle Snap

flower fairy

Gnome

Big Bad Wolf

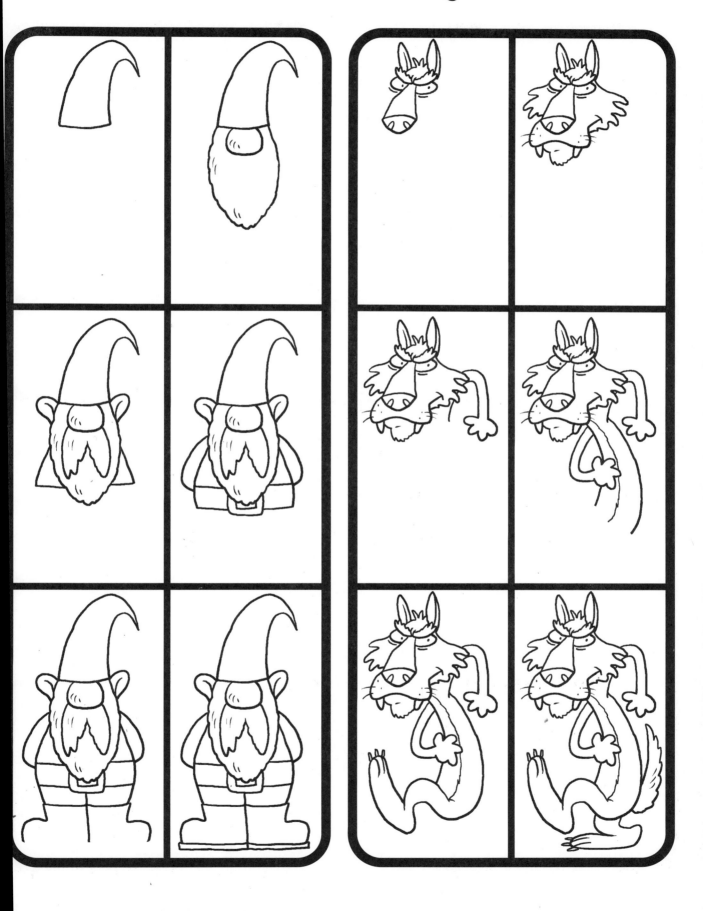

Snotter

Centaur

Thunder Bird

Three-headed ogre

Cave Troll Dwarf Lady

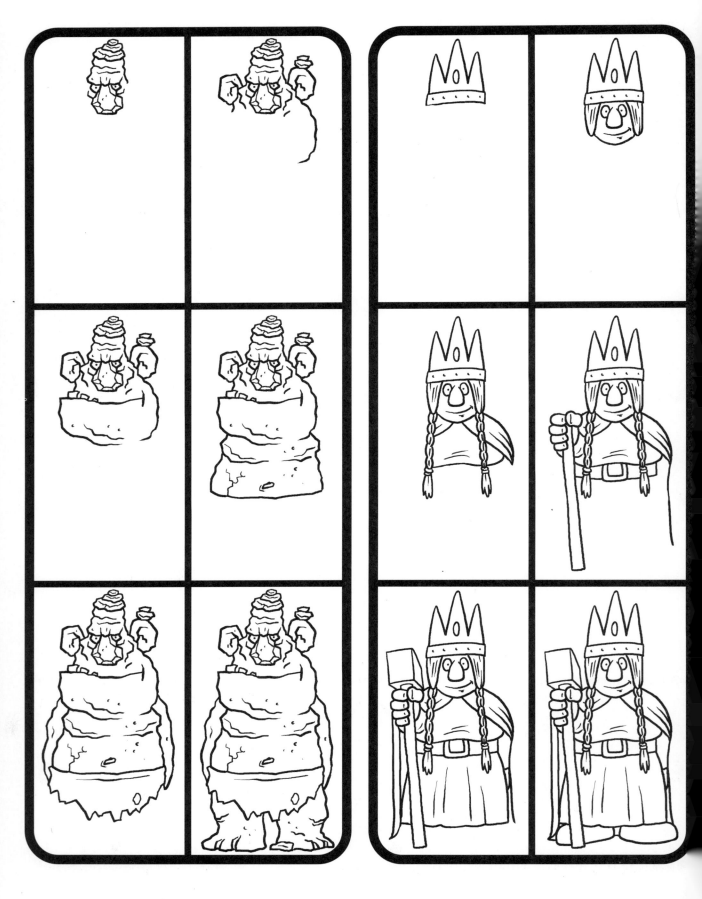

Elf Queen

Barbarian

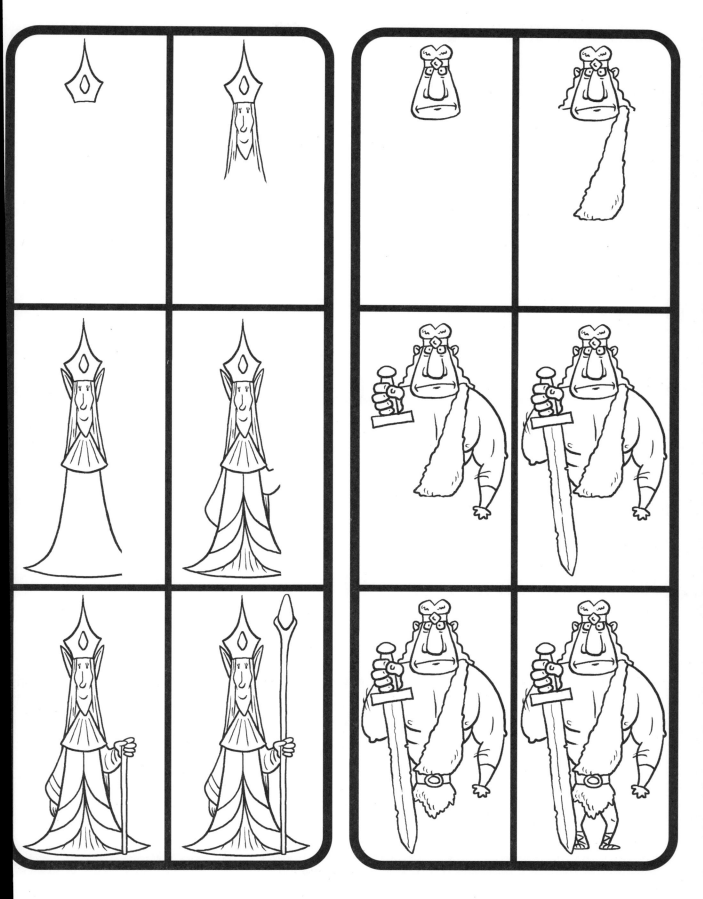

Unicorn

King Poseidon

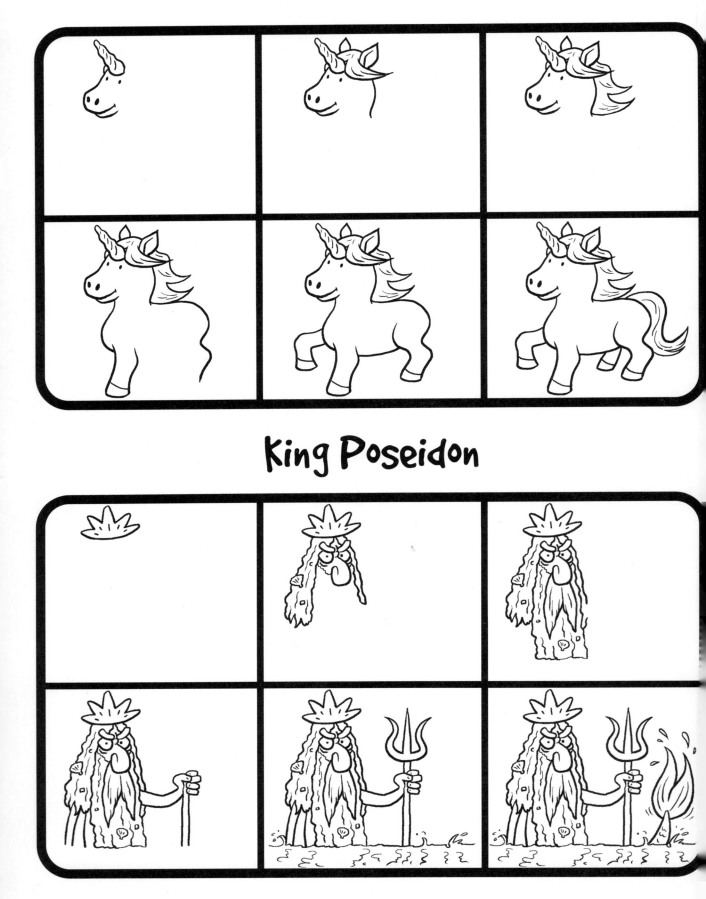

Lesser-spotted Snotter

Giant Worm

Hob Goblin

Tree Lady

Wizard King   Big Foot

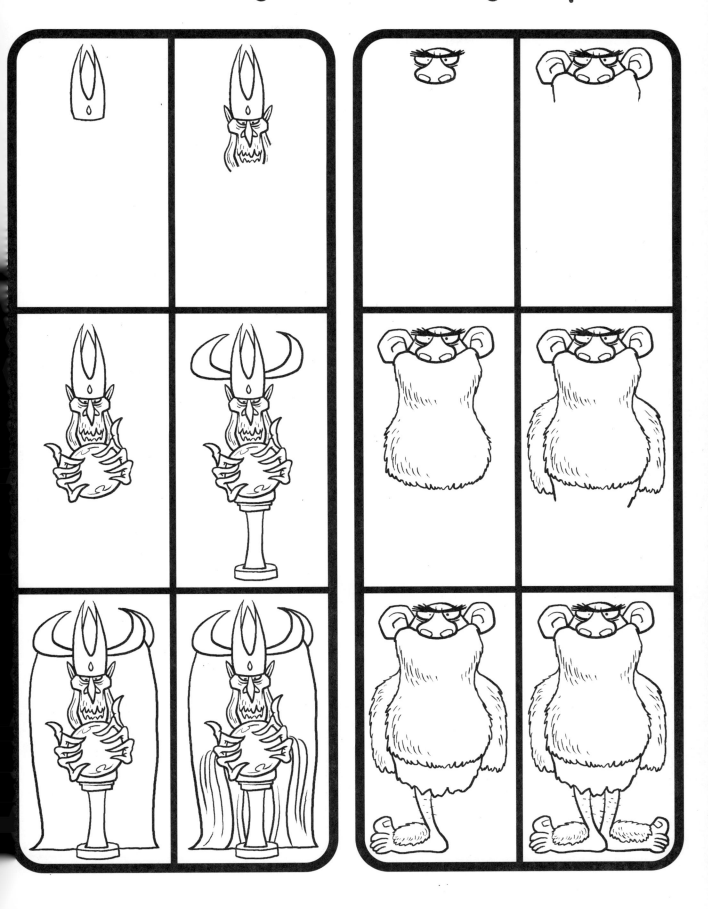

Wood Troll Bogeyman

corn fairy

cyclops

Mug Flump

Will'o'Wisp

Sphinx

Griffin

Mountain Troll   Sea Troll

White Witch

Princess

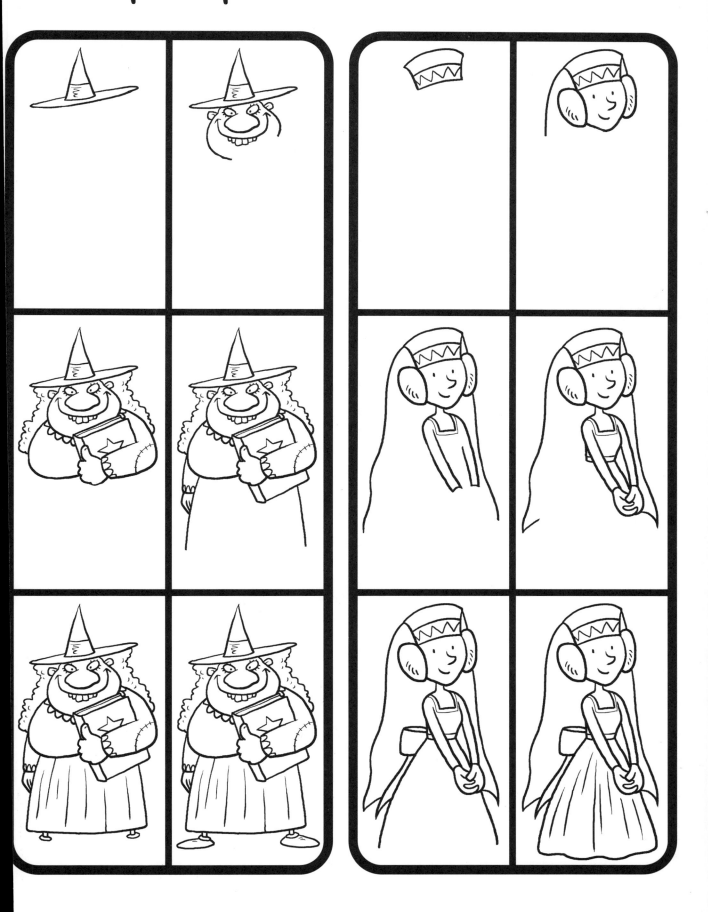

Fairy King

Unifaun

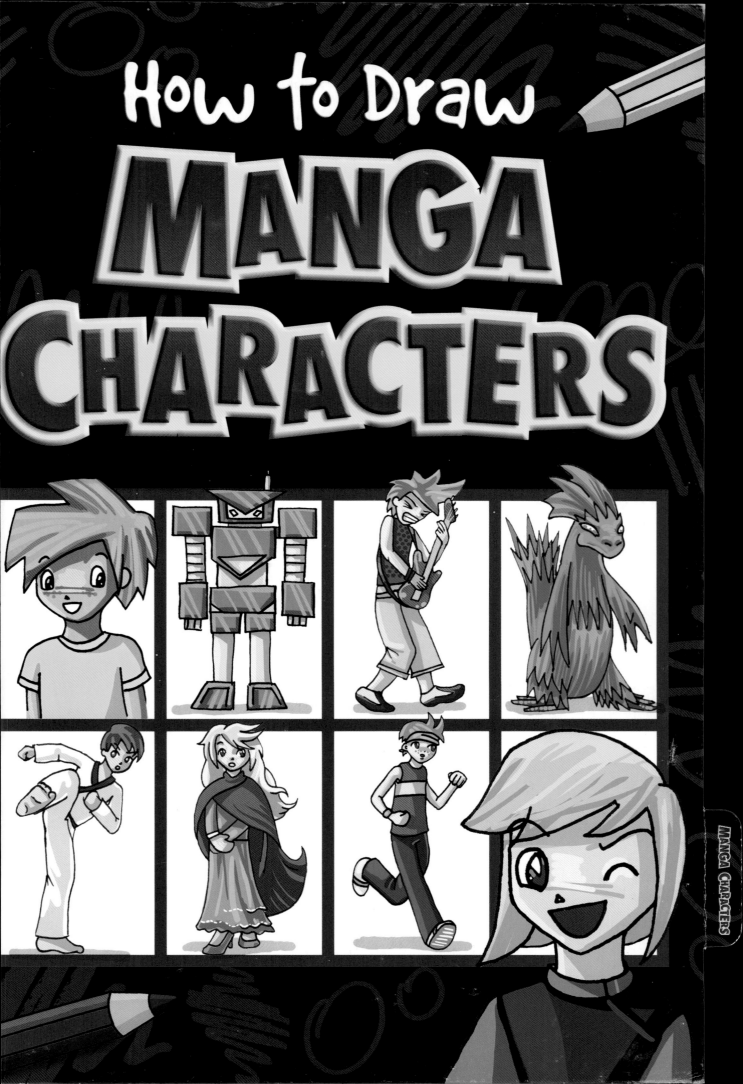

How to Draw
MANGA CHARACTERS

Ponytail

Young Girl

Teddy cuddle   # Happy Girl

School Girl

Trendy Girl

catsuit   # Skipping

Dancing

Cool Girl

Sleepyhead   curly Hair

Thumbs Up

Annoyed

Laid Back

Shy Girl

Braids

School Boy

Soccer Player

Angry Boy

Grumpy Boy

Relaxed

Trendy Boy

Cool Boy

Smart Boy

Waving

cookies

Yo-yo

Attitude

Skater

Shy Boy   # Bandana

Hoody

Ready to Go

Magical Women   Business Woman

Dancer   Athletic Woman

Racer   Walker

Karate Girl   Japanese Lady

Psychic

Winter Woman

Mother   # Archer

Smart Lady　　Party Woman

Smart Guy   Relaxed Dude

Karate

Runner

Arms Folded

Elf Archer

Shock

Wink

Tongue out

Pleased

Interested

Shy

Rocker   Robot

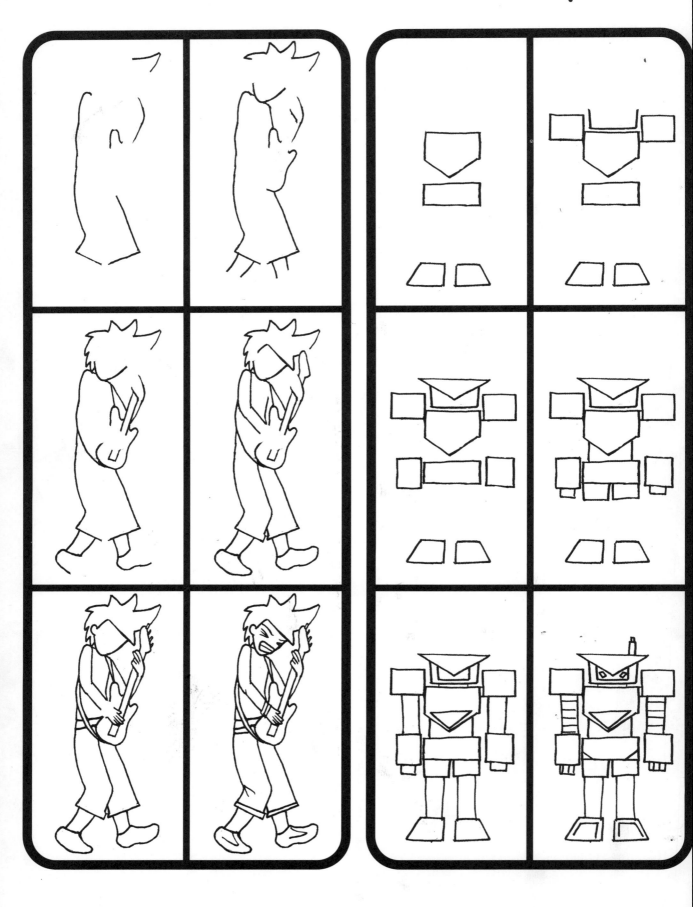

Leader　　cool Dude

fire Storm   firefoxy

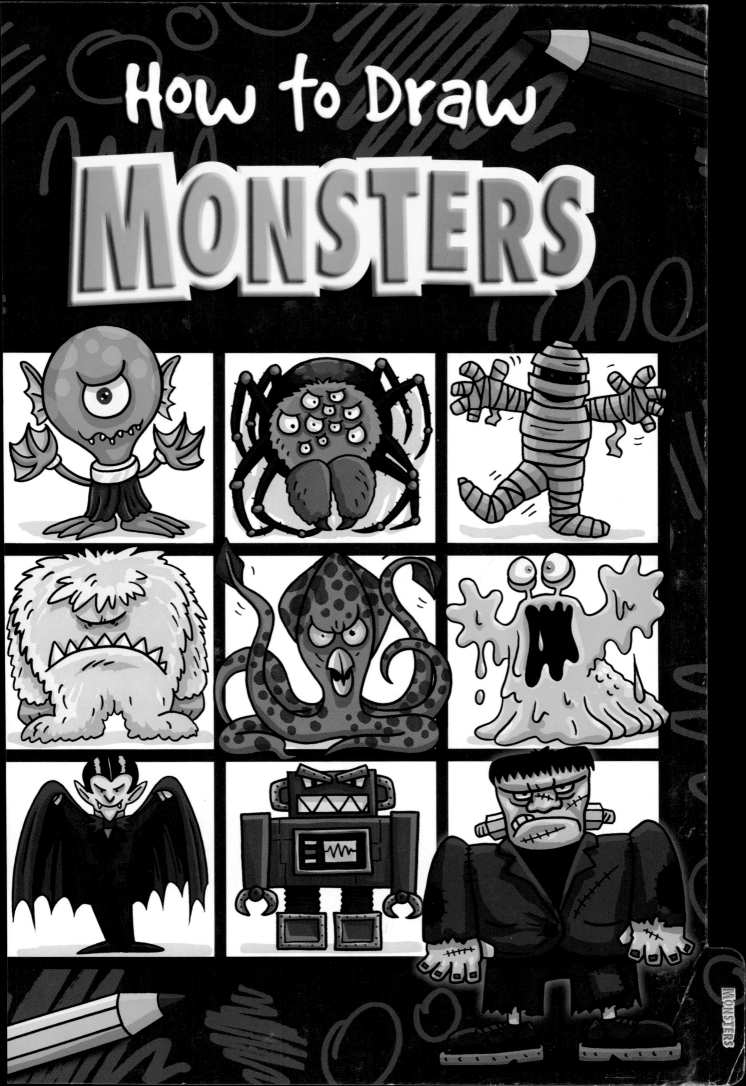

Snozz

Gargoyle

Snorky

Gumph

Jarred

crab

Nessie

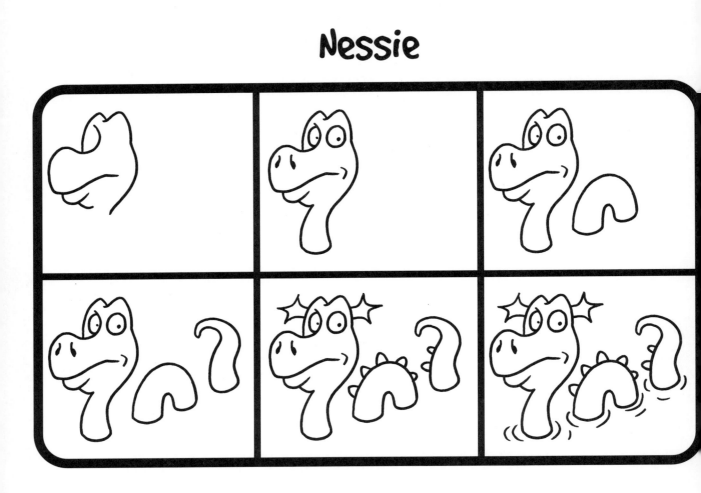

Matilda

Eyeball

Sloppy

Trog   # Hairy

Medusa

Hag

Bull

Snout

Rough

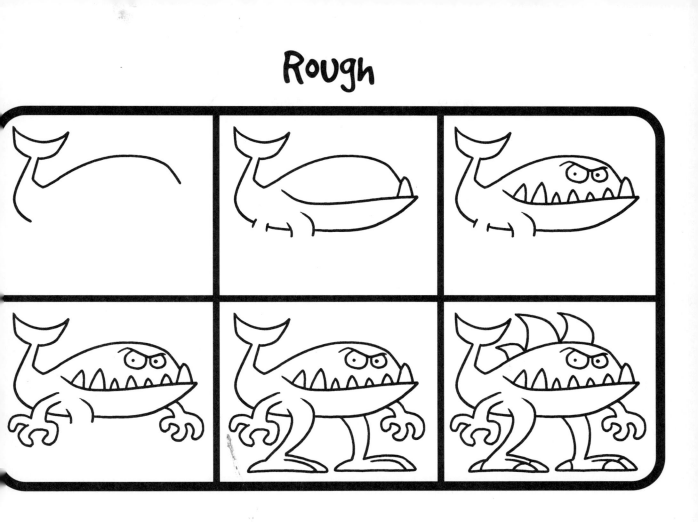

Troll-In-The-Box

Batty

Snurkle

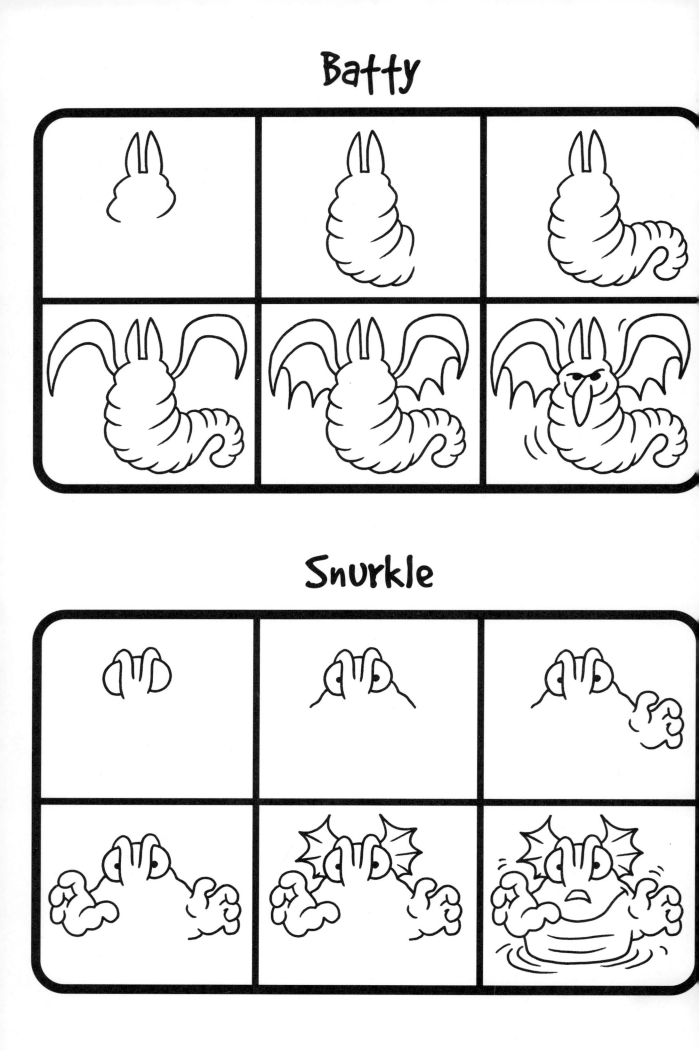

Mertle

Spider

Shaggy

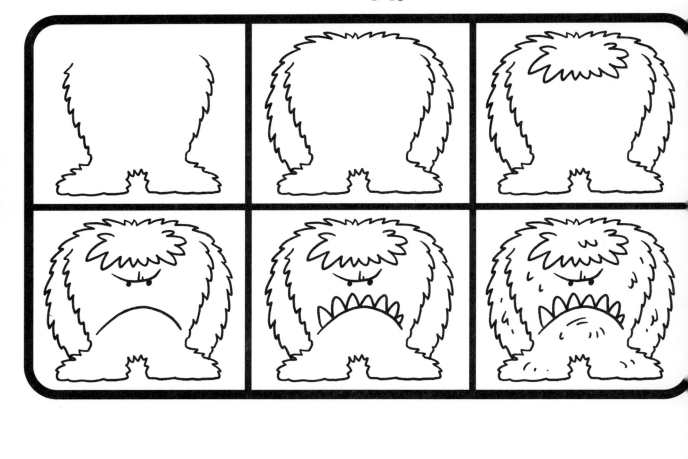

Wavy

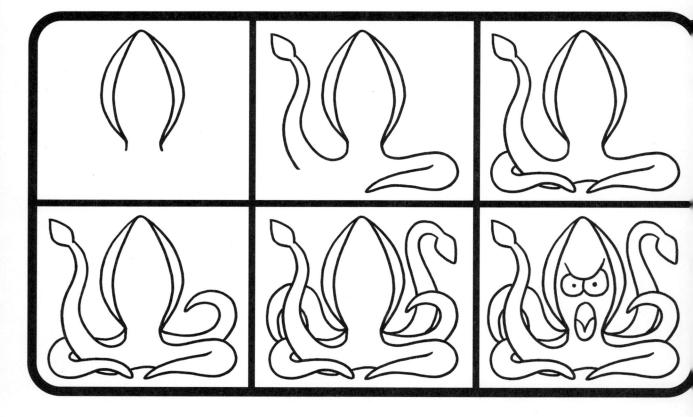

Pet

Vampire

Rah

Blob

Dev   # Rock

Slimey

Slug

flokk

Gumble

Warty

Dragon

Ted

Smelly

colly

Nun

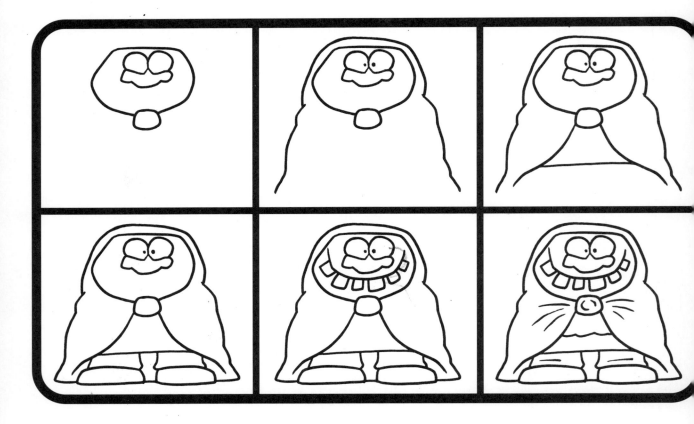

Sharky

Larry

Potty   Verm

Horn

Tree

Mad Monster

Mummy

Big one

Bendy

Eavesdrop

Squabble

Skull

Snail

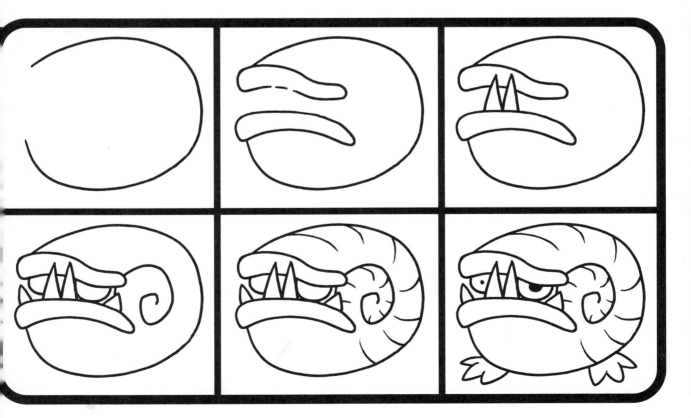

Rambo   Bolt

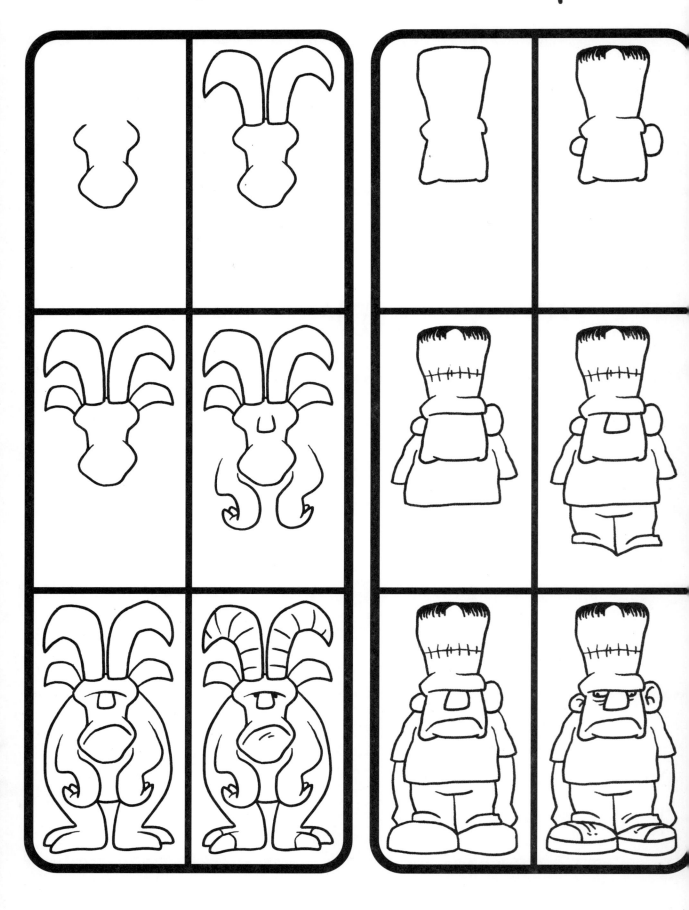

cyclops

Glum

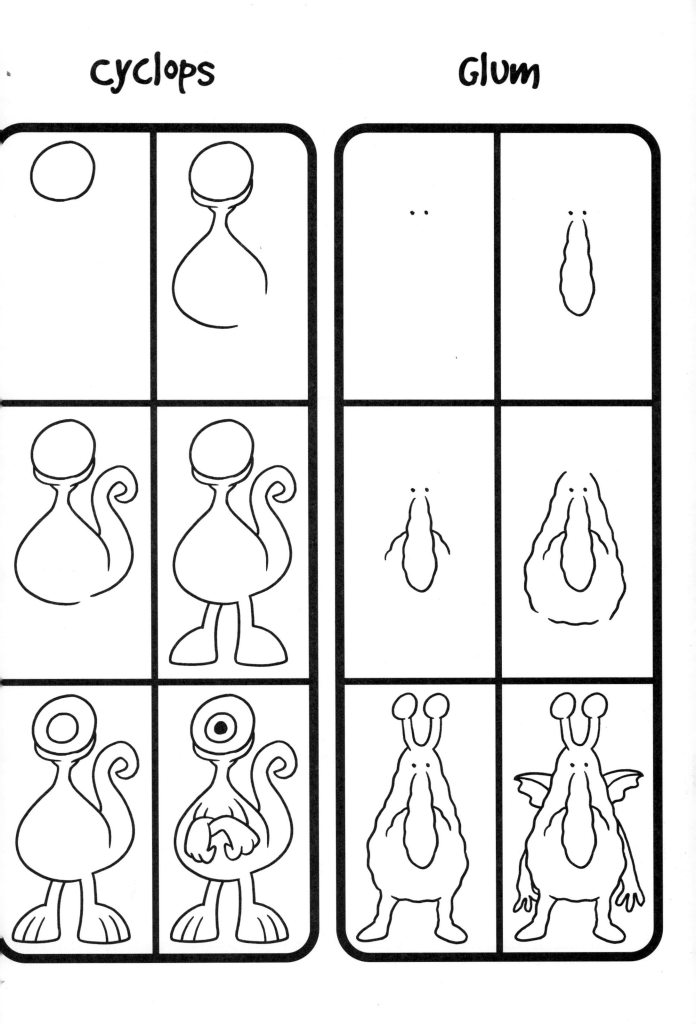

Scary

Witch

Exterminate   Vanilla

Google

Johnny